EARLY KEYBOARD INSTRUMENTS

VIOLET GORDON WOODHOUSE playing her harpsichord, made in 1912 by Gaveau of Paris under the direction of Arnold Dolmetsch.

Photograph by Herbert Lambert.

EARLY
KEYBOARD INSTRUMENTS

FROM THEIR BEGINNINGS TO
THE YEAR 1820

BY

PHILIP JAMES
of the Victoria and Albert Museum

BARNES & NOBLE, Inc.
NEW YORK
PUBLISHERS & BOOKSELLERS SINCE 1873

First Published in the United States, 1970
by Barnes & Noble, Inc.

ISBN 389 04082 7

Reproduced and Printed in Great Britain by
Redwood Press Limited
Trowbridge & London

PREFACE TO 1970 EDITION

In 1930 when Early Keyboard Instruments first appeared, the interest in old keyboard instruments and their music was in its infancy. Since then the revival has gathered pace so that today the harpsichord has its virtuoso solo performers and the continuo in performances of eighteenth century oratorios and choral music is commonly played on the harpsichord rather than on the piano. Public collections of old instruments are now maintained in playing order (even if they are not played) and the national collection at South Kensington has not only been put in order and re-arranged but is supported by a repertoire of recorded music of the period played on the contemporary instruments and by a printed catalogue of the collection.

Musicologists have not been idle in the intervening years and valuable research work has been done and the results published in books by authors including Donald Boalch, Raymond Russell and Frank Hubband.

Early Keyboard Instruments by Philip James now reprinted in facsimile remains a standard work of reference. It is illustrated with over sixty plates taken from instruments in public and private collection as well as from printed material. In addition it contains a list of over two hundred makers and sellers of keyboard instruments working in the British Isles up to the year 1820.

PHILIP JAMES

Feb. 12, 1970.

PREFACE TO 1930 EDITION

THERE is no doubt that we are witnessing to-day a revival of the early keyboard instruments. The knowledge that so much of the music now played on the pianoforte was written for the virginals, harpsichord, or clavichord, has created a natural desire to hear the music composed for these instruments as it would have been played. Lofts have been ransacked and sale-rooms invaded to rescue them from their undeserved limbo, and it is good to know that modern craftsmen are succeeding in recapturing their lost tones and their forgotten shapes. Their history necessarily demands divagations into the wider subject of musical history, and it is as a contribution towards this vast study that this slight work is offered.

The approach has therefore been from an historical rather than a technical viewpoint, and while the researches of A. J. Hipkins, G. Kinsky, C. Sachs, F. W. Galpin, and other pioneers, must inevitably form the basis of this book, an attempt has been made to co-ordinate their various discoveries and to add anything that has come to light since the publication of their works. The admirable new edition of " Grove " has, of course, been constantly at my side. The text aims at being a general survey, but numerous references are given to original sources in the form of footnotes to which the dry bones of the subject have been confined as far as possible. The period covered starts with the immediate ancestors of the keyed instruments, while a suitable *terminus ad quem* is provided by the introduction of iron into the frame of the pianoforte in the year 1820. By this date the older keyed instruments were no longer used, and after it the development of the pianoforte becomes so rapid and so complex that it forms a study in itself.

Whilst our chief interest in the early instruments is as a legacy of our musical past, it cannot be forgotten that in the days when mass-production was unknown the individual attention of the craftsman was by its very nature reflected in the thing he made: choice materials and fine proportions were the natural concomitants of skilled workmanship. The illustrations to this book leave this beyond doubt. It is well that they are now considered desirable—together with Chippendale chairs and Chelsea porcelain—for their preservation is thus made more certain and the curiosity of the musician is more easily gratified.

A list of English makers, including foreigners working in England, has been added as an appendix: it is the first of its kind and therefore admittedly incomplete, but it may serve to help owners of undated instruments to find an approximate date. Any corrections to or omissions from it will be welcomed.

His Majesty the King has graciously allowed me to reproduce Vermeer's " Lady at the Virginals " at Windsor Castle and also the " Gothic " piano on loan at the Victoria and Albert Museum. I am indebted to numerous friends and correspondents whose help and information has contributed largely towards the completeness of the text; especially to Mr. Arthur Hill, whose collection of instruments, prints, press cuttings, and other valuable documents has been generously placed at my disposal; to Mr. Francis Buckley, without whose unremitting energy in searching old London and provincial newspapers and directories the Appendix of makers' names would have been sadly deficient; and to Mr. Ambrose Heal, who has supplied me with many interesting details from his important collection of trade-cards. My thanks are also due to the following who have sent me photographs or allowed me to reproduce objects in their possession: His Grace the Duke of Rutland, Lord Sackville, Capt. the Hon. R. Legh, Capt. E. Broadwood, Mrs. G. Crawley, Capt. L. Twiston Davies, Miss E. Hipkins, Mr. G. D. Hobson, Mr. Herbert Lambert, Mr. N. Lloyd, Mr. V. Pilkington, Mr. B. C. Prichard, Mlle. G. Thibault, Messieurs M. & A. Salomon, Messrs. Batsford Ltd., the proprietors of *The Collector*, Messrs. Rushworth and Dreaper; and the authorities of the British Museum; the Victoria and Albert Museum; the Royal College of Music; the Sir John Soane Museum; the Lady Lever Art Gallery; the Musée Instrumental du Conservatoire, Brussels; the Metropolitan Museum, New York; the Grand Ducal Library, Weimar; and the Essex Institute, Salem, Mass. I have been allowed by Messrs. Novello to reproduce two blocks from Hipkins' work on the pianoforte.

I am also grateful to Mr. J. Morley for the use of his library and to Col. O. B. Harter for the excellence of those photographs which he has taken. My wife has helped me considerably with the Index. The very numerous correspondents who have sent me notes about their instruments must allow me to thank them collectively.

Philip James.

Chesham Bois, Bucks.
April 1930.

CONTENTS

LIST OF ILLUSTRATIONS

Plates

b

FIGURES IN TEXT

A SELECT BIBLIOGRAPHY

LIST OF THE MORE IMPORTANT WORKS TO WHICH REFERENCE IS MADE AND OF
OTHER AUTHORITIES CONSULTED

NOTE.—*The abbreviated titles by which some of these books are cited in the text and
notes are added in brackets after the full titles.*

GENERAL WORKS

MUSICAL HISTORY

VIRDUNG, S. *Musica getutscht und aussgezogen.* Illus. 1511. (Facsimile reprint.
Berlin: Gesellschaft für Musikforschung. *Publikation älterer praktischer und theoret-
ischer Musikwerke Vorzugsweise des XV. und XVI. Jahrhunderts.* Band XI. 1882.)
(Virdung)

CERONE, P. *El Melopeo y Maestro.* 1613.

MERSENNE, M. *Harmonie universelle.* Illus. 1636-37. (Mersenne)

KIRCHER, A. *Musurgia universalis.* 2 vols. Illus. 1650.

BURNEY, C. *The present state of music in France and Italy.* 2nd ed. 1773.

BURNEY, C. *The present state of music in Germany, the Netherlands, and the United Provinces.*
2 vols. 1773.

HAWKINS, Sir J. *A general history of the science and practice of Music.* 5 vols. 1776.

BURNEY, C. *A general history of music.* 4 vols. 1776-89.

HUYGENS, C. *Musique et musiciens au XVIIe siècle. Correspondance et œuvre musicales de
C.H. Publiées par W. J. A. Jonckbloet et J. P. N. Land.* 1882.

Oxford History of Music. 6 vols. 1901-05. (*Oxf. Hist. Mus.*)

HISTORY OF INSTRUMENTS

PRAETORIUS, M. *Syntagma musicum.* Tom. II. 1618-19.

PRAETORIUS, M. *Theatrum instrumentorum seu sciagraphia.* Illus. 1620.

RIMBAULT, E. F. *The pianoforte; its origin, progress, and construction.* Illus. 1860.
(Rimbault)

HIPKINS, A. J. *A description and history of the pianoforte and of the older keyboard stringed
instruments.* Illus. 1896. (Hipkins)

GALPIN, F. W. *Old English instruments of music.* 2nd ed. Illus. 1911. (Galpin)

SCHLESINGER, K. *A bibliography of musical instruments and archaeology.* 1912.

RUTH-SOMMER, H. *Alte Musikinstrumente.* 2nd ed. Illus. 1920.

SACHS, C. *Handbuch der Musikinstrumentenkunde.* Illus. 1920. (Sachs: *Handbuch*)
BRANCOUR, R. *Histoire des instruments de musique.* Illus. 1921.
NEUPERT, H. *Vom Musikstab zum modernen Klavier.* 2nd ed. Illus. 1926.
HAYES, G. R. *Musical instruments and their music,* 1500-1750. 1928-[in progress].

MISCELLANEOUS

LONDON: Patent Office. *Abridgments of specifications relating to music and musical instru-
    ments. A.D. 1694-1866.* 2nd ed. 1871.
BRUNI, A. *Un inventaire sous la Terreur. Etat des instruments de musique relevés chez les
    émigrés et condamnés.* 1890. (Bruni)
PIERRE, C. *Les facteurs d'instruments de musique.* 1893.
BRICQUEVILLE, E. de. *Les ventes d'instruments de musique au XVIIIe siècle.* 1908.
The Musical Antiquary. 1909, etc. (*Mus. Antiq.*)
DOW, G. F. *The arts and crafts in New England,* 1704-1775. 1927. (Dow)

WORKS ON PARTICULAR GROUPS OF INSTRUMENTS

MEDIAEVAL. PRE-KEYBOARD

GERBERT, M. *De cantu et musica sacra.* 2 vols. Illus. 1774.
BOTTÉE DE TOULMON, ——. *Dissertation sur les instruments de musique employés au moyen-
    âge.* 1844. (Article in Paris: Société Royale des Antiquaires de France.
    Mémoires, xvii, 60-168.) (Bottée de Toulmon)
COUSSEMAKER, E. de. *Essai sur les instruments de musique au moyen âge.* Illus. 1845.
    (Articles in *Annales Archéologiques dirigées par Didron ainé,* iii, etc.)
TRAVERS, E. *Les instruments de musique du quatorzième siècle d'après Guillaume de Machaut.*
    1881. (Article in Paris: Sociétés de Beaux-Arts des Départements. *Réunions,*
    v.) (Travers)
RIAÑO, J. F. *Critical and bibliographical notes on early Spanish music.* Illus. 1887.
    (Riaño)
PRIDEAUX, E. K. *The carvings of mediaeval musical instruments in Exeter cathedral church.*
    Illus. 1915. (Prideaux)

SPINET, VIRGINAL, HARPSICHORD, AND CLAVICHORD

ADLUNG, J. *Musica mechanica organœdi.* 1768. (Adlung)
BURBURE, L. de. *Recherches sur les facteurs de clavecins et les luthiers d'Anvers, depuis le
    seizième jusqu'au dix-neuvième siècle.* 1863.
VAN DER STRAETEN, E. *La musique aux Pays-Bas avant le XIXe siècle.* 8 vols. Illus.
    1867-88. (Van der Straeten)

ENGEL, C. *Some account of the clavichord with historical notices.* 1879. (Articles in *Musical Times*, xx.) (Engel, *Mus. Times*)

VAN DER STRAETEN, E. *Charles-Quint musicien.* 1894.

VILLANIS, L. A. *L'arte del clavicembalo.* 1901.

DE LAFONTAINE, H. C. *The King's Musick. A transcript of records relating to music and musicians* (1460-1700). (1909.) (De Lafontaine)

FLOOD, W. H. G. *Dublin harpsichord and pianoforte makers of the eighteenth century.* Illus. 1910. (Article in *Journal of the Royal Society of Antiquaries of Ireland*, xxxix.) (Flood)

VAN DEN BORREN, C. *The sources of keyboard music in England.* (1913.)

DALE, W. *Tschudi the harpsichord maker.* Illus. 1913. (Dale)

DOLMETSCH, A. *The interpretation of the music of the XVIIth and XVIIIth centuries revealed by contemporary evidence.* (1915.) (Dolmetsch)

JAMES, P. B. *The decoration of old keyboard musical instruments* Illus. 1927. (Article in *Old Furniture*, i.)

PIANOFORTE

PARIS: Exposition Universelle, 1855. *Notice sur les travaux de MM. Erard, facteurs de pianos et harpes.* Illus. (c. 1855.)

LONDON: International Exhibition, 1862. *List of pianofortes . . . exhibited by J. Broadwood & Sons, London. With an historical introduction, etc.* 1862.

RIMBAULT, E. F. *The pianoforte; its origin, progress, and construction.* Illus. 1860. (Rimbault)

WALLACE, Lady G. M. *Letters of distinguished musicians.* 1867.

PONSICCHI, C. *Il pianoforte, sua origine e sviluppo.* 1876. (Ponsicchi)

BRINSMEAD, E. *The history of the pianoforte.* Illus. 1879.

HIPKINS, A. J. *A description and history of the pianoforte and of the older keyboard stringed instruments.* Illus. 1896. (Hipkins)

DICTIONARIES

WALTHER, J. G. *Musicalisches Lexicon.* 1732. (Walther)

GRASSINEAU, J. *A musical dictionary.* 1740. (Grassineau)

DIDEROT, D., and ALEMBERT, J. *Encyclopédie, ou dictionnaire raisonné des sciences, des arts, et des metiers.* 1751-65. *Recueil de planches . . . 4ième livraison.* Illus. 1767. *Supplément.* 1776-77.

REES, A. *The cyclopaedia.* 39 vols. 1819.

VIOLLET-LE-DUC, E. *Dictionnaire raisonné du mobilier français . . . à la Renaissance.* Tome 2. Illus. 1871.

HAVARD, H. *Dictionnaire de l'ameublement et de la décoration.* 4 vols. (1887-90.) Illus.

SACHS, C. *Real-Lexikon der Musikinstrumente.* 1913.

MACQUOID, P., and EDWARDS, R.   *The dictionary of English furniture*.   Vol. 3.   Illus.
   1927.   (Dict. Eng. Furniture)
GROVE, Sir G.   *Grove's dictionary of music and musicians*.   3rd ed.   Edited by H. C.
   Colles.   5 vols.   Illus.   1927-28.   (Grove)

CATALOGUES OF COLLECTIONS

PUBLIC

Ann Arbor.   STANLEY, A. A.   *Catalogue of the Stearn collection of musical instruments* [at
                  the University of Michigan].   1918.
Berlin.   SACHS, C.   *Sammlung alte Musikinstrumente bei der staatlichen Hochschule
                  für Musik zu Berlin*.   Illus.   1922.   (Sachs: *Berlin Catalogue*)
Boston.   BOSTON: Museum of Fine Arts.   *Bulletin*, No. 91.   *The Leslie-Lindsey
                  collection of musical instruments* [*formerly the Galpin collection*].
                  Illus.   1917.
Brunswick.   SCHROEDER, H.   *Verzeichnis der Sammlung alte Musikinstrumente im
                  Städischen Museum*.   Illus.   1928.
Brussels.   MAHILLON, V. C.   *Catalogue descriptif et analytique du Musée Instru-
                  mental . . . du Conservatoire Royal*.   2nd ed.   4 vols.   Illus.   Gand,
                  1893-1912.   (Brussels Catalogue)
Christiania.   CHRISTIANIA: Norsk Folkemuseum.   *Saerudstilling*, II.   Fett, H.
                  Musikinstrumenter Katalog.   1904.
Copenhagen.   HAMMERICH, A.   *Das musikhistorische Museum zu Kopenhagen.
                  Beschreibender Katalog*.   Illus.   1911.
Frankfort-on-   FRANKFORT - ON - THE - MAIN: Stadtisches Historisches Museum.
the-Main.   Epstein, P.   *Katalog der Musikinstrumente*.   Illus.   1927.
London.   DONALDSON, Sir G.   *Catalogue of the musical instruments and objects
                  forming the Donaldson Museum . . . the Royal College of Music*.   Illus.
                  (1898-99.)
London.   LONDON: Victoria and Albert Museum.   Engel, C. A.   *A descriptive
                  catalogue of the musical instruments in the South Kensington Museum*.
                  2nd ed.   Illus.   1874.   (Engel)
Manchester.   WATSON, H.   *The Royal Manchester College of Music.   Catalogue of the
                  Henry Watson collection of musical instruments*.   Illus.   1906.
Milan.   GUERINONI, E.   *Gli strumenti musicali nel Museo del Conservatorio di
                  Milano*.   Illus.   1909.
Munich.   BIERDIMPFL, K.   *Die Sammlung der Musikinstrumente des bayerischen
                  Nationalmuseums*.   1883.
New York.   NEW YORK: Metropolitan Museum of Art.   *The Crosby Brown
                  collection of musical instruments of all nations.   Catalogue of keyboard
                  instruments*.   Illus.   1903.

Paris. CHOUQUET, G. *Le musée du Conservatoire National de Musique. Catalogue raisonné des instruments.* 1875.
Stuttgart. STUTTGART: Württembergisches Landesgewerbemuseum. Josten, H. H. *Die Sammlung der Musikinstrumente.* Illus. 1928.
Vienna. VIENNA: Kunsthistorisches Museum. *Publikationen aus den Sammlungen für Plastik und Kunstgewerbe*, III. Schlosser, J. *Die Sammlung alter Musikinstrumente.* Illus. 1920.
Washington. WASHINGTON: Smithsonian Institution. *Bulletin*, 136. Densmore, F. *Handbook of the collection of musical instruments in the United States National Museum.* Illus. 1927.

PRIVATE

BODDINGTON, H. *Catalogue of musical instruments, principally illustrative of the history of the pianoforte. The property of H. B. . . . formerly the collection of J. K. Pyne.* Illus. 1888.
STEINERT, M. *The Steinert collection of keyed and string instruments.* 1893.
KINSKY, G. *Musikhistorisches Museum von W. Heyer in Cöln [now the Musikwissenschaftliches Institut, Leipzig University]. Katalog. Erster Band.* Illus. 1910. (Kinsky)
SAVOYE, L. *Catalogue [vente] des anciens instruments de musique . . . composant l'ancienne collection Léon Savoye. Vente . . . 13 juin 1924.* 1924.
SKINNER, B. [*A typewritten catalogue of the keyboard stringed instruments in the collection of the late Miss Belle Skinner, Holyoke, Mass.*] Illus. 1928.
MOFFATT, H. C. *Illustrated description of some of the furniture at Goodrich Court, Herefordshire, and Hamptworth Lodge, Wiltshire.* Illus. 1928.
RUSHWORTH & DREAPER, LTD. *The R. & D. collection of antique musical instruments and historical manuscripts.* Liverpool. Illus. n.d.
BROADWOOD, JOHN, AND SONS, LTD. *The Broadwood collection of antique instruments; forerunners of the modern pianoforte.* Illus. n.d.

EXHIBITION CATALOGUES

LONDON: International Inventions Exhibition, 1885. *Guide to the loan collection and list of musical instruments . . . etc.* 2nd ed. 1885.
DALE, W. *Brief description of spinets, virginals, harpsichords, clavichords, and pianos, shown in the Loan collection of the International Inventions Exhibition, 1885.* (c. 1885.)
VIENNA: Internationale Ausstellung für Musik- und Theaterweisen, 1892. *Die internationale Ausstellung . . . Herausgegeben von C. Schneider.* Illus. 1894.
LONDON: Musicians' Company. *An illustrated catalogue of the music loan exhibition . . . at Fishmongers' Hall, June and July, 1904.* Illus. 1909.
MEYER, K. *Katalog der internationalen Ausstellung " Musik im Leben der Völker," 4. Juni— 28. August, Frankfurt am Main, 1927.* Illus. 1927.

COLLECTIONS OF REPRODUCTIONS

BONANNI, F. *Gabinetto harmonico.* Illus. 1722.

WILLEMIN, N. X. *Monuments français inédits pour servir à l'histoire des arts depuis le VIe siècle jusqu'au commencement du XVIIe.* 2 vols. Illus. 1839.

HIPKINS, A. J., and GIBB, W. *Musical instruments, historic, rare, and unique.* Illus. 1888.

SAUERLANDT, M. *Musical instruments in pictures.* Illus. 1922.

MORECK, C. *Die Musik in der Malerei.* Illus. (1924.)

LONDON: Victoria and Albert Museum. *A picture book of keyboard musical instruments.* Illus. 1929.

TEXT

TO MY FATHER AND MOTHER

CHAPTER ONE

§1. INTRODUCTION—THE ORIGIN OF THE KEYBOARD

MUSIC differs from the other arts inasmuch as it is the expression of the imagination in a medium that is transient and intangible. While the painter covers his canvas with pigments and the sculptor shapes the stone to his will the musician has to draw upon an inexhaustible supply of discrete proportionable sounds.[1] A system of notation has been devised to ensure the permanence of Music just as Poetry is permanent by virtue of the letters in which it is written, but to attain to their full emotional significance both Music and Poetry must be represented in sound. The reader of poems, however, only needs his own voice for the utterance of the words, whereas the musician is dependent upon various instruments for the production of sequential and simultaneous sounds which form the foundation of music as we know it in Europe to-day; for, as Sir Hubert Parry[2] says, "the modern European system is the only one in which harmony distinctly plays a vital part in the scheme of artistic design. . . . All other schemes in the world are purely melodic. . . . In melodic systems the influence of vocal music is paramount: in modern European art the instrumental element is strongest." The instruments which existed before the emergence of harmony were used for the most part to accentuate the dance-rhythms of primitive and semi-civilized races, and later to support the voice in singing either by doubling the melody or by adding a few simple intervals. But the gradual evolution of music from rhythm through melody to primitive harmony[3] is a vast study in itself and

---

[1] I am indebted to Mr. A. W. Wheen for the following wholly satisfying definition of music: " Music is imaginative expression by means of an inexhaustible system of discrete proportionable sounds, sequential and simultaneous, emotionally significant."

[2] Sir C. H. H. Parry, *The Art of Music*, p. 19, 1893.

[3] The *organum* of Hucbald dates from the ninth century, but no real progress towards harmony was made until the thirteenth century—a period distinguished not only by the culmination of the art of stained glass, the rise of Gothic architecture, and the beginnings of Italian painting, but also by important advances in music, *e.g.* the emergence of a time-system and its notation.

we need only know that, although in each of these three stages instruments were used, it was not until the days of pure polyphony—or " woven " music—were past, and the absorption of composers in choral music was spent, that there was an opportunity for instrumental as opposed to vocal music to flourish and for the harmonic sequence of chords to rank equally with contrapuntal music.

Among the influences which contributed towards the development of instrumental music during the sixteenth century were the rise of secular music; [1] the activities of Monteverdi and the other monodists, who introduced their revolutionary harmonies at the close of the century and busied themselves with the cultivation of the solo voice and the crude instrumental technique necessary for its accompaniment; and thirdly the improved social conditions accompanying the Renaissance which not only broadened domestic life but encouraged intercourse with foreign countries. This development was naturally influenced by the character of the new music so that two types of instruments in particular came to be improved, the bowed instruments because they could support or replace the solo voice and the keyboard instruments because they were suitable both for the playing of chord-sequences and for the accompaniment of the voice. The former must be dismissed as being outside our scope, but the latter—with the notable exception of the organ—will form the substance of this book. The organ, however, cannot be entirely ignored, as with it alone the early history of the keyboard is associated.

Although the organ of the ancients is of eastern origin the keyboard is a purely western device and is confined to Europe, for the invention of a series of balanced key-levers is said to be due to the ingenuity of the Greek mathematician Ctesibius of Alexandria, whose water-organ of *circa* 250 B.C. has been described in detail by his pupil Hero. [2] The architect Vitruvius [3] has also given us an account of its construction in the first century of our era. After this the keyboard seems to have disappeared completely [4]—perhaps

[1] Music, like the other arts, had hitherto been chiefly in the service of the Church, but the existence of secular music in the Middle Ages, as proved by the works of Guillaume de Machault, is too often overlooked.

[2] In the *Pneumatica*, printed in vol. i of Teubner's edition of Hero, 1899.

[3] Vitruvius Pollio, *De Architectura*, bk. x, cap. xiii. Fortunately these rather nebulous descriptions of the hydraulus were supplemented in 1885 by the discovery of a small model, made of baked clay, found in the ruins of Carthage. For a full description of this, and a working model, see Galpin's article " Notes on a Roman Hydraulus," in *The Reliquary*, 1904, p. 152: it is also figured in Grove, article *Hydraulus*.

[4] For about a thousand years there was a box of movable slides instead of a keyboard. These slides were placed beneath the holes leading to the pipes and they were perforated so

because of the severe condemnation by the early Christians of Roman customs and contrivances—until it was virtually re-discovered in the eleventh century when the keys were as large as the treadle of a knife-grinder's machine and were struck by the organist's clenched fist which was protected by a leather glove. About a hundred years later keys are found on the small portative organs which are figured in contemporary illuminated manuscripts, but it was not until the fifteenth century that the chromatic notes were placed in a row higher and separate from the naturals.[1] So far the history of the keyboard has been inseparable from that of the organ, unless we include the hurdy-gurdy [2] which, however, did not influence the development of the keyboard in any way as it was soon superseded by the organ: it was not the prototype of any other instrument unless the strange *Nürmbergisch Geigenwerck*, described by Praetorius,[3] is counted as its descendant, and although it was intimately associated with the arcadian concerts of the French aristocracy in the eighteenth century, its revival under the name *vielle* for the *fête champêtre* was musically insignificant. Although in the thirteenth century this instrument did not have keys but little slides, comparable with those on the early organs, which were pressed in to stop the strings at the desired point, it is interesting to note that this action foreshadowed the mechanism of the first stringed instrument to which a keyboard was added, *i.e.* the clavichord. It seems, however, almost certain that it was not the primitive hurdy-gurdy but the monochord from which

that the wind was admitted when they were pushed in and excluded when they were pulled out again. The tongue of each slide which projected from the side of the box was marked with a letter to show the player which note it controlled.

[1] A good example of an early chromatic keyboard is seen in the picture of St. Cecilia which forms one of the panels of the famous Van Eyck altar-piece at Ghent. The inside of this polyptych was painted by Hubert Van Eyck between the years 1424 and 1426.

[2] It appeared in the tenth century under the name Organistrum and later it was known as the Symphony. When it was revived in the eighteenth century it was made in the shape of a viola d'amore, guitar or lute, and in common with these instruments it was often enriched with elaborate carving and inlay: sometimes the bodies of old lutes and guitars were converted into hurdy-gurdies. The sound is produced by the friction of a rosined wheel against the stretched strings—an action comparable with that of the bow of a violin: the player turns this by means of a handle with his right hand while with his left he presses the keys which, having little tongues of wood on the end, stop the strings just as the fingers do on the neck of a bowed instrument. Of the six strings two, known as *chanterelles*, were melody strings tuned in unison: these were stopped by the twenty-three keys. The other strings made a drone which could be tuned to the key of G or D. For further information see Galpin, cap. vi, and Kinsky, i, 374-6.

[3] See p. 39.

the clavichord developed because for a long time these two names were interchangeable.

The thirteenth century is the traditional date for the application of a keyboard to a stringed instrument, and it is not unlikely that this development, which was to be of such great consequence, was effected in this most remarkable period when a spirit of adventure was abroad and art was universal rather than individual. We are now at the threshold of our subject, but a brief examination must be made of the instruments of this period which naturally lent themselves to so important a mechanical improvement.

§2.   MEDIAEVAL INSTRUMENTS THAT PRECEDED THE INVENTION OF THE KEY-
BOARD—PSALTERY, DULCIMER, ÉCHIQUIER

The latent music in a series of tightly stretched strings was probably revealed to primitive man when he shot his arrow from a taut bow-string, and it needed but little ingenuity on his part to construct from this simple idea an instrument which would gratify his desire for music. In fact, in almost all savage and semi-civilized races we find an instrument consisting of strings of various materials stretched over some kind of hollow resonance-box or sound-board.[1] There are, however, three ways of exciting sound from a stretched string, namely, by plucking, striking, or stroking it—actions in modern times performed respectively by the jacks of the harpsichord, the hammers of the piano, and the bow of the violin. The first two methods only concern us here. After being used on the instruments of prehistoric peoples they formed the actions of the psaltery and dulcimer—instruments both of ancient history and the Middle Ages from which sprang, on the one hand, the group of keyboard instruments with plucked strings, and on the other the pianoforte. We shall see that the clavichord stands apart in a class by itself, both by reason of its origin and its action.

The histories of the psaltery and dulcimer have always been difficult to

---

[1] The usual division of musical instruments into the three classes of percussion, wind, and strings is hardly complete, and the main groups of the exhaustive classification made for the Musée du Conservatoire at Brussels are quoted as being more accurate, viz. Sonorous Substances, Vibrating Membranes, Wind, and Strings. Uncivilized nations have instruments representative of the first three of these groups also, *e.g.* rattles and cymbals, drums and tom-toms, and simple pipes made of bamboo, etc. Stringed instruments with a finger-board belong to races of more developed culture, and those played with a bow are the least common.

distinguish, especially in their early stages, because the plectra often used by the player instead of his fingers for *plucking* the strings of the former cannot always be differentiated from the little hammers or rods used for *striking* the strings of the latter, and also because representations of them before the Middle Ages are extremely rare. The records we have show that neither were known to the Egyptians or Assyrians,[1] but that the Chinese and Hebrews used the psaltery [2] which is, like the lute and several other European instruments, undoubtedly of Asiatic origin. Next, it is included amongst the instruments of the Greeks, whence comes its name; [3] although the Greek psaltery was more like a species of lyre—their favourite stringed instrument of which they had several forms. Their Music, together with the rest of Greek culture, was inherited by Rome, and there are numerous references to the Roman *psalterium*: but apart from the interest of their actual existence the instruments of the ancients belong to experimental times and we can proceed to the society of the Middle Ages when Music, the youngest of the arts by so many centuries, leaves the stage of theory and speculation and demands performance first as the servant of the cosmopolitan Church, and later as mistress of the arts, courted and honoured by the pagan princes of the Renaissance. Here again the westward march of oriental influences is observed, for not only can the origin of several European instruments be traced to the occupation of Spain by the Arabs, who in their turn had assimilated Persian culture since their conquest of that country, and had been in fruitful contact with the Chinese since the eighth century, but also the Crusades " raised Venice to the pinnacle of her wealth and glory . . . and flooded Europe with luxuries and crafts imported or imitated from the East." [4]

[1] The much-discussed representation of an instrument on the Assyrian bas-relief in the British Museum, figured and described by Engel (*Music of the most ancient nations*, p. 44) as a dulcimer, is not accepted by Galpin (p. 66), who holds that it is a trigon or triangular harp. But see also E. A. Wallis Budge, *Assyrian sculptures in the British Museum*, Pl. xix, 1914, or H. R. Hall, *La sculpture babylonienne et assyrienne au British Museum*, Pls. xxxviii and lxii, 1928: even from these better preserved reliefs it is impossible to identify the instruments accurately.

[2] The *yang-kin* in China and the *koto* in Japan are still popular. The Hebrew *nebel*, latinized as *nablum*, is considered to have been a psaltery of semicircular shape played by the hand: it is depicted in a MS. of the ninth century at Angers (reproduced in Engel, p. 92), and in the bas-relief of the eleventh century from the Abbey of St. Georges de Boscherville, Normandy, now in the Museum at Rouen (Engel, p. 113).

[3] The word Ψαλτήριον means an instrument of which the strings are twitched or plucked.

[4] G. M. Trevelyan, *History of England*. The allusion to Venice is significant, as we shall show later that it is probable that here the keyboard stringed instrument first reached a

In the Middle Ages the psaltery was in general use from the ninth to the sixteenth century, and was especially popular not only as an ecclesiastical instrument, but also in the bands of minstrels attached to royal courts and noblemen's houses: [1] in the *chansons de geste*, too, its praises are sung, and it was evidently used for accompanying the voice as the lute was at a later date, for Nicholas, the poor scholar of Chaucer's *Miller's Tale*, had one in his hostelry which he used in this way:

> And above all ther lay a gay sautrie
> On which he made on nyghtes melodie,
> So swetely, that all the chambre rong:
> And *Angelus ad virginem* he song.

It appears in almost every list of mediaeval instruments and there are innumerable representations of it in the illuminated manuscripts, stained glass, sculpture, and paintings of this period. It was made in several shapes and sizes. The earliest were triangular and rectangular [2] and had from eight to twenty strings stretched over a resonance-box, unlike the harp of which the strings are free. The former rested point downwards on the player's arms so that the hands were left free to pluck the strings, the latter was held upright or laid flat on the knee (Pl. II). One of the most common

state of real mechanical efficiency: and the Venetians by their trade with the Levant introduced Saracenic arts and sciences into Europe. They were doubtless familiar with the Persian form of psaltery, called the *santir* (Pl. I).

[1] An interesting ms. in the Public Record Office, printed by the Roxburghe Club (*Manners and household expenses of England*, pp. 140 *ff.*, 1841), gives a list of payments made to the many minstrels who played before Edward I at Whitsuntide, A.D. 1306. Amongst them are Gilletin le Sautreour and Janyn le Sautreour who received xl*s.* and 1 marc respectively. It is interesting to note that at this period minstrels had their ranks—of which the highest was " King "—and were paid each according to his degree.

[2] Illustrations of these early types are figured in Abbot Gerbert's *De cantu et musica sacra*, in which he reproduces drawings from a ms. of the ninth century, which was destroyed in a fire in 1768 at the monastery of St. Blasius in the Black Forest. The rectangular psaltery here has ten strings and is " in modum clypei quadrati ": see also the example of the eleventh century in Galpin, Pl. xii. There were numerous slight modifications of these two forms and the following examples are worth examination: Figures of the Elders of the Apocalypse round the tympanum of the Gate of Glory at Santiago de Compostela (thirteenth century), the Cantoria or Choir Gallery made for the cathedral at Florence by Luca Della Robbia (fifteenth century). Casts of both are in the Victoria and Albert Museum. There are several forms in the famous manuscript at the Escorial, known as *Cantigas de Santa Maria* (thirteenth century), which is reproduced in colour in Grove, and in innumerable other illuminated mss., also in many pictures by the Italian artists, especially in representations of the Coronation of the Virgin who is often surrounded by an angelic choir.

forms was elaborated from the triangular form and was fancifully known in Italy as the *strumento di porco*, owing to its supposed likeness to the profile of a pig: it was in general use from the thirteenth to the sixteenth century, and the strings were plucked either by plectra or by the fingers (Pls. III and IVʙ).[1]

An examination of many representations of the instrument shows that from the fourteenth century the strings were sometimes grouped three to each note [2]—a trichord system used in the piano to-day—and that about a century later a new wing-shaped psaltery appears, which was sometimes strung on both sides of the sound-board.[3] This type is of special interest to us as it was probably to a psaltery of this shape that a keyboard was first applied, thus producing a primitive form of the harpsichord. On the Continent the double psaltery lasted into the eighteenth century,[4] thus long outliving the other forms which died a natural death after the birth of their own offspring—the keyed psaltery, or *clavicembalo* as it was called in Italy, where it probably originated.[5] A modern survival of the psaltery is the zither, a very popular instrument in Germany and the Tyrol.

[1] Other good representations of this type are in an English Psalter of the thirteenth century in Munich Royal Library; Reid ms. 75 in the Victoria and Albert Museum; Memling's triptych of Christ and angels (Nos. 778-780) at Antwerp; Fra Angelico's Madonna dei Linajuoli at the Uffizi; the sculptured figures on the canopy of Bishop Bronescombe's tomb in Exeter Cathedral (reproduced in Prideaux, Pl. xvi); carved figures on the roof of Manchester Cathedral; the stained glass at Beauchamp Chapel, Warwick (reproduced in *Archaeologia*, lxi, Pl. 96), and Rouen Cathedral, etc. Early in the sixteenth century an exaggerated variation of this type appeared in Italy: scalloped edges are a feature of its extravagant design (Pl. V). For additional examples, see Salting ms. 1223 (Victoria and Albert Museum) and the paintings by Gaudenzio Ferrari in the Sanctuario at Saronno.

[2] Psalteries of this type are figured in Orcagna's fresco—the Triumph of Death—in the Campo Santo, Pisa, and in the same painter's Coronation of the Virgin in the National Gallery, also on a Spanish altar-piece reproduced by Riaño (fig. 56).

[3] An unique English example is among the sculptures on the canopy of Bishop Brones-combe's tomb at Exeter (Pl. IVᴀ). For a full description see Prideaux, p. 31, where it is conveniently named the double psaltery. Another representation, with strings on one side only, is seen in a copy in the Prado of a lost original altar-piece, usually known as The Fountain of Living Water, which is attributed to one of the Van Eycks.

[4] It was known at this period as the *Spitzharfe* (Germany), *Arpanetta* (Italy), and *Vleugelharp* (Netherlands). It had strings on both sides of the sound-board and stood upright on the ground (Pl. VI). The Turkish *kanoon*, known in Europe in the Middle Ages as the canon, is also of this shape; but the strings are usually of gut instead of metal.

[5] Galpin, p. 65: "In the thirteenth century to some form of Psaltery the name Cembalo or Cymbal was given [as well as salterio], apparently because the resonance of its strings resembled the bell-chimes called Cymbals, which were so popular in all European countries at that time."

So much for the origin of the keyboard instruments with plucked strings. The dulcimer must now be briefly studied as it is the prototype of the piano-forte in all its various forms which, however they may differ in appearance, all have strings which are struck. The mediaeval dulcimer, also of Eastern origin, resembled the psaltery in appearance, usually being trapeze-shaped, and as we have already remarked it is easy enough to mistake the little hammers or rods, held one in each hand, for the plectra of the psaltery. This resemblance, however, hardly accounts for a noticeable dearth of representations of it in contemporary paintings and sculptures,[1] and it has been suggested that the word " psaltery " was used to denote both instruments. The sweetness of its tone, from which its name was derived,[2] was perhaps responsible for the fact that, unlike the psaltery, it did not disappear with the introduction of keyboard music: and by this quality it earned an encomium from Pepys who, after visiting a puppet-show [3] at Covent Garden, wrote: " Here among the fiddles I first saw a dulcimer played on with sticks, knocking of the strings and is very pretty." The English dulcimer was usually of three octaves, having two strings tuned in unison for each note in the key of D major. The German *hackbrett*, however, was tuned to the chromatic scale. An additional effect was given to the " knocking of the strings " if the leather was thin and hard at one end of the hammers and thicker and softer at the other: this change in the quality of tone is not possible, or desirable, in the piano, but the earliest square pianos, of which the small hammers were similarly covered with thin leather, produce a tone

---

[1] In addition to the Byzantine ivory book-cover of the twelfth century (Pl. VII) at the British Museum (Egerton 1139) and the English examples noted by Galpin (p. 64), the follow-ing mediaeval examples are recorded: the beautiful miniature from the ms. *Le Livre des Echecs Amoureux*, fol. 65, in the Bibl. Nat., Paris (Pl. VIII); a Tree of Jesse from a MS. breviary in the Royal Library, Brussels (reproduced in P. Lacroix, *The arts in the Middle Ages*, fig. 157, London, 1870); a Madonna at Perugia painted by Boccati (reproduced in Miss A. Kemp-Welch's article " Musical Instruments in Italian pictures " in *The Monthly Review*, vii, 1902).

[2] The Latin name *dulce melos*, sweet melody, discovered by Bottée de Toulmon (p. 123), became *doucemelle* in old French, *e.g.* in the fifteenth-century poem quoted by Hipkins (p. 53); but the general name for it in France has always been *tympanon*, which must not be confused with *tympanum*, the Latin word for the kettle-drum. Both words are descriptive of a striking action (Gr. τύπτειν). There was also a Celtic instrument, the tympan, which Galpin (pp. 67 *ff.*) believes was a kind of dulcimer. In England the word " dowcemere " appears as early as *c.* 1400. The Italian name—*salterio tedesco* (Pl. IX)—hints that it was much used in Germany, where it was the *hackbrett*, literally a butcher's chopping-board which it resembled in shape.

[3] It seems to have been used regularly for such performances, as Grassineau says: " The instrument is not much used except among puppet-shows."

which tells that, apart from their mechanism, they are little more than keyed dulcimers. Like the hurdy-gurdy it became at the beginning of the eighteenth century a plaything of the French [1] aristocracy (Pl. X), afterwards to be cast aside and become part of the stock-in-trade of itinerant musicians, who lived on the charity of such benefactors as that full-blooded cleric Parson Woodforde: more than once he " gave 3*d.* to an old man that played on the dulcimer." It survives to-day as the *zimbalom* in the bands of the Magyar gipsies.

The immediate ancestors of the two distinct groups of keyboard instruments have now been described, but before we close this chapter mention must be made of an instrument of which the exact nature has yet to be discovered: there are several variations of its name—in French, *eschaquier d'Engleterre*, or *échiquier*, and in Spanish *exaquir*. The references to it that have so far been found are so few and so brief that it is impossible to say more than that it was probably a stringed instrument with a keyboard. The word also means a chessboard and it has been suggested that either the alternating black and white keys or a chequered decoration of the case gave rise to the name. Support is given to this theory by the occurrence of the word *shachtbret* in the well-known list of rules for the Minnesingers [2] and, in spite of strong objections on etymological grounds to the use of this word as the German for *échiquier*, this seems the only possible explanation. [3] While we must admit that for want of any constructive evidence in this matter we can only make destructive criticism, we must also dismiss the ingenious suggestion made by Galpin, [4] that the checks of the *échiquier* are nothing but

[1] It was popularized by the performances of Pantaleon Hebenstreit, who made a much enlarged instrument on which he performed before Louis XIV in 1705. The delighted monarch suggested that the instrument should be named the Pantaleon. See Walther, and Grove, articles *Hebenstreit* and *Pantaleon*.

[2] These rules by Eberhard Cersne, dated 1404, are preserved in the Nationalbibliothek at Vienna; they were edited by F. X. Wöber, Vienna, in 1861.

[3] See Sachs, *Real-Lexikon*, 125-6. He maintains that the use of *shacht* for *schach* is not supportable, and makes the plausible suggestion that Cersne being a Westphalian, and therefore in close proximity to the highly developed music of the Netherlands, used the Netherlandish word *schacht*, *i.e.* quill (as in *kielflügel*—the usual German for " harpsichord ") but Prof. E. Weekley has written this to me: " No doubt *schachtbret* is merely an accidental spelling, excrescent *t* being as common in German as in English; *cf.* ' the game of chests,' which was literary English in the seventeenth century. I feel sure that *Schachtbret* is merely an error for *Schachbrett*, and that the instrument was identical with the *eschaquier d'Engleterre*."

[4] Galpin, p. 121, referring to the word *échiquier*, says: " it is most likely, however, that it refers to the jacks, which, appearing in a row across the sound-board, suggested the idea of chessmen, which was enhanced by the action of ' checking ' or repulsing the strings as

the jacks of a virginal or harpsichord.   So far all the earliest references to this obscure instrument date from the fourteenth century.   In 1360 Edward III gave an *eschequier* to King John of France, when he was his prisoner: [1] and in about 1370 it is mentioned in a poem [2] by Guillaume de Machault, musician, poet, and chronicler at the court of Philippe Le Bel, King of France.   It is here called *l'eschaqueil d'Engleterre*, and it has consequently been suggested that the origin of the keyboard instruments with plucked strings is English and not Italian, as we have hitherto believed it to be, but this is the only reference in which it is described as being definitely English, and we know only one allusion in English records to an instrument with which it may perhaps be identified. [3]   We hear of it in the household accounts [4] for 1385 of Philip the Bold, Duke of Burgundy, who two years later receives a request from his brother-in-law, John of Aragon, to send him an *exaquir*.   In the sixteenth century the *archiquier* is included amongst the instruments of Charles V, [5] in whom we see the culmination of the princely patronage

they rose to pluck them.   We know that the old English word *chaw* has given us *jaw* . . . so the *check* of the Echiquier has become the jack of the English virginal and harpsichord." Prof. Weekley, referring to this passage, remarks that " the derivation of the word jack from check seems fanciful and the phonetic parallels adduced have no force, *e.g.* the real origin of jaw is probably Fr. *joue*, cheek (*cf.* paw, O.F. *poue*).   The applications of the personal name 'jack' to mechanical devices are very numerous."

    [1] See A. Pirro, *Les clavecinistes*, pp. 1-7, for this and several other interesting references.

    [2] In Travers the passage of his long rhymed chronicle, *La Prise d'Alexandrie*, which contains an enumeration of all the contemporary musical instruments, is quoted in full.   It is also found in a verse by Eustache Deschamps (*c.* 1378):

> " Ne je n'y ay phisicien,
> Fors Pantiau le musicien,
> Qui jeue, quant je l'en requier,
> De la harpe et de l'eschiquier."

    [3] In the roll of accounts of the receipts and expenses of Robert de Braybroke, Bishop of London, the following payment in the year 1392-3 is noted: " Datum cuidam ludenti super le chekker apud Stebbenhith [Stepney] de precepto domini iij*s.* iiij*d.*"   See the article by W. H. Grattan Flood in *Music and Letters*, vi, p. 151, 1925.

    [4] France: Ministère de l'Instruction Publique (B. et H. Prost, *Inventaires mobiliers et extraits de comptes des ducs de Bourgogne*, II, 2me fasc., p. 196, 1909).   " Payé le 20 décembre [1385], 12 fr. à dam Gilles de Rouais, religieux de l'église de Saint-Martin de Tournay, pour un instrument nommé eschiquier que Mgr. a fait acheter de lui et mectre en sa chapelle."   The use of the word *nommé* suggests that the instrument was not in common use at this period.

    [5] This important reference, discovered by Van der Straeten (vii, 40), is discussed by Hipkins (p. 54), who mentions " an *espinette organisée* in the great Music Exhibition which took place at Vienna, in 1892, that closing up like a draughtboard, the name of exaquir, échiquier, or exchequer, might have been appropriate to."

STRINGED INSTRUMENTS

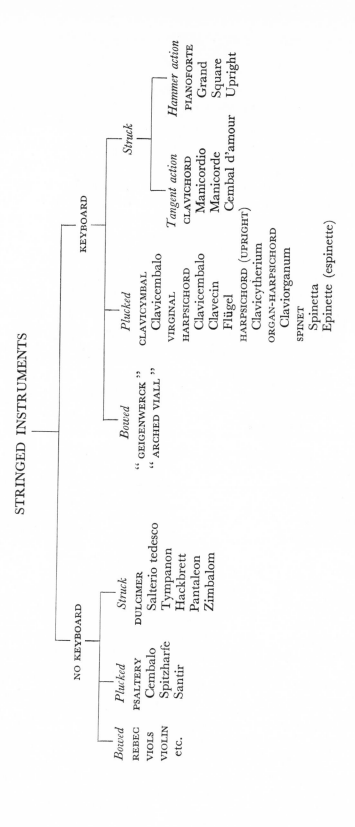

NO KEYBOARD

Bowed
REBEC
VIOLS
VIOLIN
etc.

Plucked
PSALTERY
Cembalo
Spitzharfe
Santir

Struck
DULCIMER
Salterio tedesco
Tympanon
Hackbrett
Pantaleon
Zimbalom

KEYBOARD

Bowed
" GEIGENWERCK "
" ARCHED VIALL "

Plucked
CLAVICYMBAL
Clavicembalo
VIRGINAL
HARPSICHORD
Clavicembalo
Clavecin
Flügel
HARPSICHORD (UPRIGHT)
Clavicytherium
ORGAN-HARPSICHORD
Claviorganum
SPINET
Spinetta
Epinette (espinette)

Struck

Tangent action
CLAVICHORD
Manicordio
Manicorde
Cembal d'amour

Hammer action
PIANOFORTE
Grand
Square
Upright

given to music by the House of Burgundy throughout the Middle Ages.[1] The reference to John of Aragon is important, as the King describes the instrument as *semblant d'orguens qui sona ab cordes*; and the only instruments which can be said, with a stretch of the imagination, to look like an organ but sound by means of strings are the upright harpsichord, usually known by its Latin name *clavicytherium*, and the *claviorganum*—a spinet or harpsichord with a small organ attached which is operated by the same keyboard.[2] So if only some more evidence were available, it might be found that the evolution of the *clavicembalo*, by the addition of a keyboard to the psaltery in the fifteenth century, had been forestalled a century earlier by the *échiquier*, or even that they were one and the same instrument.

Before the earliest keyboard instruments are more fully discussed in the next chapter reference should be made to the table on the preceding page. This is intended to show the relationship of the instruments which already have been and will be mentioned, and to prevent the confusion which is sometimes caused by the use of several names for one instrument.

[1] E. Van der Straeten, *Charles Quint, musicien*, p. 24.
[2] Pirro, *op. cit.*, tells us that the Duke of Lorraine bought an *échiquier organisé* in 1511.

CHAPTER TWO

THE CLAVICHORD

THE monk Guido d'Arezzo, who flourished early in the eleventh century, has not only been more often quoted by musical historians than any other writer of antiquity, but has also been credited with many more outstanding reforms [1] than he actually effected, including the invention of the monochord and the clavichord. The monochord—a single vibrating string as its name implies—was a mathematical rather than a musical instrument used by the Greek philosophers, notably Pythagoras, for measuring off the intervals of the fundamental musical scale by means of movable bridges. Its use as such was encouraged by Guido,[2] and it became a tetrachord and was used as a key to the eight tones [3] of the ecclesiastical modes on which the Plain-Song of the Church was based. Soon afterwards the primitive keyboards on portative organs, to which reference has already been made, doubtless suggested themselves as a means of simplifying the clumsy system of movable bridges on the monochord, so a set of balanced key-levers was added at the end of which small blades of metal known as tangents were fixed. When the key was depressed the tangent rose, struck the string and produced a sound, at the same time measuring off the exact length of string required to produce the desired note and itself acting as a bridge. The musical possibilities of this contrivance, than which nothing could be simpler, were not, of course, realized in the thirteenth century, and instrumental music was as yet unborn, but—as we shall show presently—this early form of clavichord probably differed but little from the perfected instrument of the eighteenth century.

[1] He is known chiefly for the popularization of the stave and the invention of solmization.

[2] A drawing from a thirteenth-century illuminated MS. of Guido and Teobaldo, Bishop of Arezzo, using a monochord is figured in Gerbert's *Scriptores ecclesiastici de musica sacra*, ii, 1784, and in H. J. Hermann, *Die deutschen romanischen Handschriften*, fig. 155, Leipzig, 1924.

[3] It is interesting to learn that there were sculptured representations of the Eight Musical Tones; *e.g.* on two capitals saved from the Choir at Cluny. See V. Markham, *Romanesque France*, pp. 120 *ff.*, 1929.

This evolution of the clavichord from the monochord, as opposed to the hurdy-gurdy, is made more plausible by the fact that the name monochord stuck to it even as late as the sixteenth century; [1] this would also account for the absence of the name clavichord before the fifteenth century, when it is first found in Cersne's rules for the Minnesingers. [2] Literary references and pictorial representations are by no means common before 1500, [3] but after this date allusions to it become more frequent. Entries relating to it are found in the Privy Purse expenses of Henry VII and his queen, Elizabeth of York, for the year 1502, and in the same year on the occasion of a pageant given in Westminster Hall in honour of Catherine of Spain " twelve ladies had claricordis, [4] claricymballs, and such other." A woodcut of it appears in the first book [5] about musical instruments, which was written by a priest, Sebastian Virdung, and printed at Basle in 1511; in this woodcut, which was not reversed for the engraver, the treble keys appear to act upon the longest strings and *vice versa*—an error blindly followed by Martin Agricola [6] and

---

[1] Much confusion is caused by this interchange of names. In the Romance languages, it was always *manicordo* (Ital.), *manicorde* (Fr.), etc., while *clavicordio, clavicorde*, etc., often meant a spinet (see Hipkins, p. 58). In Scotland it was usually called *monocordis*.

[2] It has been stated that as wire drawing was first practised by one Rudolf of Nuremburg in the middle of the fourteenth century a *terminus a quo* is provided, but " recent research in this direction indicates that this claim is invalid and that the process was known before Rudolf's time. . . . There are brief references to the drawing of wire through dies in documents 900 to 1000 years old." See A. T. Adam, *Wire drawing*, 1925.

[3] The earliest reference to it in England, found by W. H. Grattan Flood, is dated 1477 (*Music and Letters*, vi, 151): and in 1483 it was deemed to be part of a minstrel's equipment, for in Caxton's translation of *Geoffrey de la Tour* Sir Geoffrey demanded of one clothed like a minstrel, " where his vyell or clavycordes were and that he should make hys craft." The earliest representation of it is a drawing in a Wunderbuch (*c.* 1440) in the Grosherzoglichen Bibliothek at Weimar (Pl. XI), where there is also a drawing of a clavicymbal. In England a wood-carving in the roof of St. Mary's, Shrewsbury (Galpin, fig. 20), and the stained glass in Beauchamp Chapel, Warwick, for which the contract was dated 1447, contain the earliest examples. Miss Prideaux (p. 31) describes the latter as a psaltery, but in the reproduction of this window (*Archaeologia*, lxi, Pl. 95) a keyboard is clearly visible.

[4] Rimbault, p. 43. The substitution of *r* for *v* is found in numerous references and does not denote, as Rimbault suggests, a different instrument. Sir W. Leighton in his *Teares or Lamentations of a sorrowfull Soule*, 1613, uses the form *claricoales*; and *claricon* is another variant.

[5] *Musica getutscht und auszgezogen*, Basel, 1511. A facsimile reprint of this very rare book was published in Berlin in 1882 (see the Bibliography, p. xiii).

[6] *Musica instrumentalis deudsch*, Wittemberg, 1528, etc. In the preface he explains that he has written this work in verse, because proverbs and rhymed books are more easily remembered by the young!

Ottmar Luscinius,[1] who wrote treatises upon music shortly afterwards. Virdung clearly favours the monochord as the origin of the clavichord, for he says: [2]

I was never able to find out who first conceived the idea of placing keys at certain points in accordance with the diatonic which struck the string exactly on the same line or point, thus producing at that point precisely the note which the diatonic naturally gives. Neither do I know who, by virtue of these keys, named the instrument the *Clavicordium*.

And again, making the popular error of claiming Guido as the inventor but repeating his opinion about its source, he writes:

I consider what Guido Aretinus called the monochord to be the clavichord.

We also learn from Virdung something about the compass of the early clavichords. The number of tones did not exceed thirty before about 1500, by which time the chromatic scale was establishing itself and the compass was increased to about three octaves, as in the earliest known clavichord which, though subsequently reconstructed, is dated 1537 (Pl. XII). About a century later it was increased to four octaves and it was not till the eighteenth century that it reached five.[3]

The action of the clavichord has already been commended for its simplicity: it is also perfectly efficient. The oblong case containing the action measured from three to six feet in length according to its compass and date of construction, and between one and a half and two feet in width: the key levers occupy the left side and the soundboard, which never extends over the keys, is on the right. On the extreme right of the soundboard, in two or more rows, tuning-pins, known as wrest-pins, are set in a block of wood—the wrest-plank—and from them the strings [4] of thin brass wire are

---

[1] *Musurgia seu Praxis musicae*, Strasburg, 1536. This book is a monument of plagiarism. Not only are all the illustrations taken from Virdung, but the text is substantially the same, having been translated into Latin. In fact, the slight defects in Virdung's woodcuts are so faithfully reproduced that it is not unreasonable to suppose that the actual woodblocks were acquired from Basle for this book by the printer at Strasburg.

[2] *Op. cit.*, E ii, v.

[3] See Sachs (Berlin Catalogue, p. 44) for an elaborate classification for the dating of clavichords according to compass, shape of key-lever, measurement of the keys and material of which they are made, arrangement of the wrest-pins, etc., etc.

[4] Each note usually had two strings tuned in unison to increase the tone, and in the eighteenth century Jakob Adlung tells us, in a detailed description of the clavichord in his

stretched, a pair for each note, first to a bridge to which they are pinned, in order that the sound-waves may be thus transferred to the soundboard, and thence to the far side and back of the case where they are fixed to the hitch-pins. The keys are not kept in position by pins but are prevented from lateral movement by a small piece of whalebone or brass, which is fixed into the back of the key-lever and fits into a little groove in the back of the case. When the key is depressed and the metal tangent strikes the string the vibration of the shorter length is damped by a strip of cloth intertwined between the short lengths which is known as " listing ": this also damps the whole string when the key is allowed to rise and the tangent falls.

A characteristic feature of the early clavichords is the action of more than one tangent upon the same string, the different notes being produced by the tangents striking the same string but at different points. They were termed fretted or *gebunden* in Germany, where the clavichord was always more popular than the jack instruments,[1] and it was not until after the introduction of equal temperament that musicians dispensed with this economy,[2] which seems so impracticable to-day. The first provision of a pair of strings for each note in about 1725, making the instrument *bundfrei* or fret-free, has erroneously been attributed [3] to Daniel Faber, organist at Crailsheim, for not only are there *bundfrei* clavichords of an earlier date,[4] but Bach's first book of " the Forty-Eight " was published in 1722. The full significance of this must not be missed, for it is often forgotten that many of the preludes and fugues in the *Wohltemperirtes Clavier*—Bach's contribution to the contro-

Musica mechanica organoedi, published posthumously in 1768, that there were sometimes three. Occasionally the lower tones only had a third string of very thin wire tuned an octave higher, as in the fine instrument by Barthold Fritz in the Victoria and Albert Museum (Pl. XV).

[1] If a census of all surviving examples were made, it would probably be found that three-quarters of them were German. It seems to have been little used in France, and most of the surviving Italian clavichords are not later than the middle of the seventeenth century. Only one English clavichord is known (Pl. XIV).

[2] These fretted clavichords, however, continued to be made throughout the eighteenth century. They had the advantage of being lighter and smaller than the larger fret-free instruments which were usually made with a stand.

[3] Walther, p. 235. This seems to be the original source for this often-quoted statement.

[4] Canon Galpin has drawn my attention to a *bundfrei* clavichord in the Henry Watson Collection at the Royal Manchester College of Music (No. 93 in the catalogue), which is dated 1700. It is of the unusually great compass, for that date, of five octaves, and there are two strings to each note. It has black naturals and ivory sharps. The case is 5 ft. by 1 ft. 9 in., and it bears the following inscription: *Fabriert von Johann Wilhelm Gruneberg Alt Branden-burg* 1700.

versy about equal temperament—were written for the clavichord. Two directly opposed views as to the instrument used for this immortal collection have recently been expressed. A brilliant harpsichordist claims,[1] with arguments of unconvincing ingenuity, that

> all these fugues are simply inconceivable in terms of the quaint and grey clavichord. . . . Why then will people persist at all costs in attributing to Bach a particular predilection for the clavichord?

We must oppose this intolerance on the grounds that Bach certainly had a " predilection for the clavichord," [2] and that he was always interested in the work of Gottfried Silbermann [3] of Dresden: besides, it must be evident immediately to anyone who has played on both instruments—to choose at random two preludes from the first book—the first in C major, or the eighth in E flat minor, that for the perfect interpretation of them no other instrument can be used, except perhaps a particularly responsive piano. In a spirited rejoinder [4] to such fanatical partisanship it is maintained that

> the Clavichord is still the only keyboard instrument capable of producing without mechanical means the sustained tones with which the compositions of J. S. Bach are so richly endowed:

but the notes of a good harpsichord can certainly be made to equal those of

[1] *The Dominant*, Nov. 1927.

[2] Bach's appreciation of the clavichord is insisted upon as an historical fact by nearly all his biographers. Forkel says: " Bach preferred the Clavichord to the Harpsichord which, though susceptible of great variety of tone, seemed to him lacking in soul ": and Spitta remarks that the clavichord " was precisely Sebastian's favourite instrument. . . . It was possible to play cantabile on it, and this cantabile style was regarded by Bach as the foundation of all clavier-playing."

[3] Silbermann, a famous maker of organs and clavichords, who was prominently connected with the introduction of the piano into Germany, also invented in 1723 a double clavichord with strings of twice the usual length to which he gave the unfortunate name *cembal d'amour*: the word *cembal*, strictly applied to the psaltery, was often used as a short form of *clavicembalo*, the harpsichord, but never for the clavichord. A contemporary drawing of the instrument is reproduced in an article by Van der Straeten (*Mus. Times*, Jan. 1924). Other special instruments are mentioned by Adlung, who says that some had a lute-stop. In these half of the blade of the tangent, which was of extra length, was covered with leather and when the stop was pulled out this part came into contact with strings. He also mentions transposing clavichords of which the pitch could be altered by means of a device for moving the keyboard, and pedal-clavichords of which an interesting specimen dated 1760 is described and figured by Kinsky (p. 45). In addition to Silbermann and Fritz, the other chief German makers during the eighteenth century were Hass, Hubert (Pl. XVI), and Carl Lemme.

[4] *The Dominant*, Feb. 1928.

a clavichord in duration of tone.[1]   There will probably never be a final settlement of this much-debated question, but it is at least a constructive suggestion that both instruments were used.   Indeed, it is not difficult to decide in many cases for which instrument a particular prelude or fugue was written, and the use of the word *clavier* as a generic term for all the keyboard instruments rather than to denote a particular one was certainly in accordance with contemporary custom.[2]   Schröter, the German musician and pianoforte designer, has given us the important information [3] that his own pupils used the clavichord for private study and the harpsichord for public performance, and this was the usual practice of Haydn [4] and Mozart.

The polyphonic texture of much of this music can undoubtedly be presented as well on a clavichord as on a harpsichord, and the fact that there is a minimum of intervening mechanism between player and strings makes for that intimate, personal relationship which is possible for those who make music by means of a bowed string.   Indeed, by virtue of this close contact with the string that characteristic and beautiful effect known as *Bebung* is produced.   This is a kind of tremulous accentuation or increase of intensity by means of a slight vibratory pressure on the key, producing a corresponding variation of pitch similar to the vibrato used by violinists. As this expressive quality is peculiar to the clavichord and should be acquired by every player of the instrument, a more detailed description of it from an instruction book [5] of the eighteenth century is not out of place:

The Bebung can be applied effectively only to a long-sustained tone, especially in compositions of a plaintive character.   It is usually indicated in the notation by these marks—

---

[1] An average figure is from five seconds in the treble to eight seconds in the bass.

[2] It was, however, used sometimes to denote specifically the clavichord, especially in conjunction with the harpsichord and piano, *e.g. Klaviere, Flügel, und Pianoforte.*

[3] *Oxf. Hist. Mus.*, v, 50.

[4] Haydn's clavichord, on which he composed the *Creation* is still in existence.   It was made by Johann Bohak in 1794 (see the author's article in *Mus. Times*, April 1930).

[5] D. G. Türk, *Klavierschule, oder Anweisung zum Klavierspielen*, Leipzig and Halle, 1789. This passage is translated and quoted by Engel in *Mus. Times*, xx, 471, and it is his translation that I repeat here.

or by the word tremolo being written over the note; and its execution is this—

In order to produce it effectually the finger must be held on the key as long as the duration of the tone demands, and the player must endeavour to increase the loudness of the tone by a gentle pressure of his finger several times repeated. It is perhaps hardly necessary to say that after each pressure the weight must be slightly relaxed, without however raising the finger entirely from the key. Moreover, everyone knows that this expression is only attainable on a clavichord, and, indeed, only on a very good one. In general the player ought to guard himself against the frequent employment of the Bebung, and if he employs it he must take care to avoid the objectionable manner of forcing the tone above its pitch by too vehement a pressure.

It was doubtless the skilful use of *Bebung* that moved Burney to record [1] his visit to Carl Philipp Emanuel Bach at Hamburg in 1772 in these words:

M. Bach was so obliging as to sit down to his Silbermann clavichord, and favourite instrument, upon which he played three or four of his choicest and most difficult compositions, with the delicacy, precision, and spirit for which he is so justly celebrated among his countrymen. In the pathetic and slow movements, whenever he had a long note to express, he absolutely contrived to produce, from his instrument, a cry of sorrow and complaint, as can only be effected upon the clavichord, and perhaps by himself.

This second son of Sebastian Bach was a well-known exponent of keyboard technique, and in his famous work on the subject,[2] in which he laid the foundation of modern pianoforte technique, he insists upon diligent practice on the clavichord for the attainment of a perfect touch:

By constant playing on the harpsichord we take to playing with one kind of tone, and the different shades of tone which can be produced even by an ordinarily good clavichord-player are completely lost.

[1] *Present state of music in Germany*, etc., second ed., ii, 269.
[2] *Versuch über die wahre Art das Clavier zu spielen*, pt. i, 1753, pts. i and ii, 1762, etc., section 17.

This view was endorsed by Burney, who tells us that when he was in Vienna he attended a musical party given in his honour by one of the court physicians where a small girl regarded as a musical prodigy performed.[1]

> All the pianos and fortes were so judiciously attended to and there was such shading of some passages and force given to others, as nothing but sensibility could produce. I enquired of Signor Giorgio, an Italian, who attended her, upon what instrument she usually practised at home, and was answered, " on the Clavichord." This accounts for her expression and convinces me, that children should learn upon that, or a Piano Forte, very early, and be obliged to give an expression to Lady Coventry's Minuet, or whatever is their first tune; otherwise, after long practice on a monotonous harpsichord, however useful for strengthening the hand, the case is hopeless.

All this evidence by contemporary writers of the practical contribution to musicianship to be gained by the study and use of this little instrument cannot be dismissed as being merely of antiquarian interest. It is true that at the present time, when our ears are dulled by the opulence of tone to which we are now so accustomed, the full appreciation of its small gentle voice would have to be acquired. It never was fitted for the concert platform or the recital but was essentially the instrument of the inner chamber, where the parson and the schoolmaster of many a German village found consolation and recreation in the music of the old masters. Happily this is again possible for there are not wanting craftsmen to-day who have recaptured the art of making the clavichord,[2] and—what is more important—a demand for it may be created if modern composers [3] continue to recognize that it should have a place among the keyboard instruments.

[1] Burney, *op. cit.*, i, 278.

[2] The reintroduction of the clavichord is primarily due to Mr. Arnold Dolmetsch, whose instruments (Pl. XVII) have not only attracted the attention of musicians but have also served to encourage other craftsmen, such as Mr. H. Tull and Mr. Herbert Lambert.

[3] The book of pieces for the clavichord entitled *Lambert's Clavichord* (Oxf. Univ. Press, 1928), recently written by Mr. Herbert Howells, shows a feeling for the distinctive qualities of the instrument and yet is expressed in a modern idiom.

CHAPTER THREE

SPINET AND VIRGINAL

THE actual date of the evolution from the mediaeval psaltery of keyboard instruments with plucked strings will never be known, for like all similar processes it was a gradual development which is probably to be assigned to the thirteenth and fourteenth centuries. As the monochord became the clavichord by the addition of tangents and keys, so at a little later date the psaltery also was given keys, and jacks took the place of the fingers or little plectra held in the hands. Again, the action was of remarkable simplicity, and again it lasted with but few improvements until the end of the eighteenth century, for the jacks of the earliest instruments only differ in insignificant details from those of the harpsichords made to-day. On the end of each balanced key-lever rests the thin flat strip of wood known as the jack: in the centre of its upper part a long narrow strip is cut out and a pivoted tongue of holly-wood inserted, on which one end of a hog's bristle presses, the other end being attached to the main body of the jack. At right angles to this tongue and fixed in it is the plectrum which projects so that when the key is depressed it plucks the string as it passes (Pl. XLI). When the key is allowed to rise the plectrum misses the string as the jack falls owing to the ingenious arrangement of the bristle which, while it keeps the tongue of wood firmly in position for its upward motion, allows it to pivot and the plectrum thus to miss the string on its return. A small piece of cloth fixed into the body of the jack a little above the level of the plectrum damps the string when the key rises to its original position[1]. The jacks are prevented from jumping right out by a strip of wood known as the jack-rail. It is padded on the inside with baize or felt and fits into slots in the sides of the case.

Instruments with this action were made in various shapes and sizes and were accordingly given different names, *e.g.* spinet, virginal, and harpsichord. The earliest examples were shaped like a recumbent harp, *i.e.* they were early specimens of the harpsichord, and they will therefore be consid-

---

[1] Some makers gave their jacks two dampers, one each side of the tongue.

21

ered in the next chapter.   This leaves the spinet and virginal, which will be studied together as the two names were used indiscriminately, one in one country and one in another, until the end of the seventeenth century, when they were both used in England to denote two different instruments.   The emergence of these keyboard instruments from an experimental state coincides with the Golden Age of music which reached its apogee in the glorious vocal polyphony of such masters as Palestrina and Orlando di Lasso; and although at this time instrumental music was completely eclipsed by the prevailing choral style, yet it was so far advanced that instruments of a high standard of craftsmanship were being made in the first quarter of the sixteenth century.   In Italy especially, where the tide of the Renaissance was now at full flood, attention was evidently given to keyboard music earlier than elsewhere,[1] and the instruments were sufficiently developed to receive the praise of Castiglione, who remarks in *Il Cortegiano*, his masterly picture of court life at Urbino written in 1514:

> all the keyboard instruments are very harmonious because they give the harmonies with great perfection, and many things can be performed on them which fill the spirit with melodious sweetness.

Fortunately we can approximately date the appearance of the spinet in Italy, as distinct from the earlier harpsichord, from a passage in the *Poetices* [2] of Julius Caesar Scaliger (1484-1558), and another [3] in a book about the organ published in 1608.   Referring to the evolution of the keyboard instruments from the psaltery, Scaliger says:

> Then plectra, points of crow-quill, were added: they evoke a more expressive sound. . . .   When I was a boy these instruments were called Clavicymbal and Harpsichord but now owing to those points of quill they call it Spinet.

The addition of crow-quills was an important change from the leather or metal plectra which had been used earlier,[4] and it was doubtless from this

[1] We remarked in the last chapter that the earliest known clavichords are also of Italian provenance.

[2] Lib. i, cap. xlviii.

[3] *Conclusioni nel suono dell' organo, di D. Adriano Banchieri, Bolognese*, Bologna, 1608.   See Grove, article *Spinet*.

[4] Mr. A. Dolmetsch, whose great experience in the restoration of old instruments enables him to speak with authority, says (p. 420): " a variety of materials have been used

improvement that the Italian name *Spinetta* arose, for the quill points are not unlike a thorn,[1] *spina*. A far less likely origin for the name is given in the passage from Banchieri which is, however, valuable rather as evidence of the introduction of an oblong spinet (*spinetta a tavola*) as opposed to the more common pentagonal and hexagonal instruments with which the Italian craftsmen are always associated [2]. He says:

> The spinet received its name from the inventor of the oblong form, Master Giovanni Spinetti, a Venetian; and I saw such an instrument in the hands of Francesco Stivori, organist of the illustrious municipality of Montagnana and it bore this inscription: JOANNES SPINETUS VENETUS FECIT. A.D. 1503.

The documentary evidence afforded by these extracts is confirmed and a little antedated by the fact that the earliest known Italian spinet by Alessandro Pasi of Modena [3] is dated 1490. This instrument, however, was of the graceful pentagonal shape called *spinetta traversa*, which is mentioned above. This was the form adopted by craftsmen in other countries, and with various modifications of outline it lasted into the eighteenth century. The Italian examples of this type are characterized by an unparalleled profusion and richness of decoration (Pls. XIX-XXI).

Only in the Netherlands was music equally developed at this period, and here too instrument-makers were experimenting with the plucked string. The reigning House of Burgundy led the way in the cultivation of music as we learn from Van der Straeten's interesting description of them[4]:

> Charles attacha donc son nom aux premières épinettes perfectionées sorties des ateliers flamands, anversois surtout. . . . Sa sœur, Eléonore—

for the plectra, the principal being quills and leather. The latter was much used in the sixteenth century; but for a century or so from about 1650 it was almost entirely superseded by quills. Leather was reintroduced in the eighteenth century, at times replacing the quills altogether. There is a marked difference between the tone-colour produced by these two materials, especially when buff leather is used. The quills give a sharp and brilliant tone, but one not so pure and sweet as that of leather."

[1] The French word *épinette*, or *espinette* in old French, has the same derivation.

[2] Sometimes the pentagonal instruments were enclosed in an oblong outer case without any attempt to fill up the empty spaces at the corners.

[3] Exhibited at Bologna in 1888.

[4] *Charles-quint, musicien*, passim. The elaborate instrument made for the Duke of Cleves (Pl. XVIII), who frequented Charles's court after marrying his niece, Marie d'Autriche, reflects the skilled craftsmanship displayed in their instruments.

qui devint plus tard une vraie artiste du chant—s'amusait déjà, en 1506 à jouer de petites bagatelles sur une épinette qui sortit d'un atelier renommé: celui d'Antoine Mors.

These instruments were probably of the oblong shape which was more popular than the transverse Italian shape, not only in the Netherlands but also in Germany where at this period it had the misleading and meaningless names *Instrument* and *Symphonia*. The use of the name *spinet* seems to have been confined to France and Italy at this date, and it is significant that there is no mention of it in Virdung who, however, describes an oblong jack instrument which he calls the *virginal*.[1] He is unable—as in the case of the clavichord—to suggest its provenance, but it is not unlikely that this name originated in England, where it was used to describe all the domestic keyboard instruments—whatever might be their sizes or shapes—throughout the sixteenth century.[2] The use of the instrument by young girls is now generally accepted as the origin of the word—a derivation supported by the fact that in all the engravings and genre pictures of musical scenes it is always a woman who stands before or is seated at the virginals (Pl. XXVII) while men play the lute, viola da gamba, etc. The earliest reference to it in England is probably in one of the " proverbs " formerly written [3] on a wall in the Manor House, Leckingfield, in the time of Henry VIII:

> A slac strynge in a Virgynall soundithe not aright,
> It dothe abyde no wrastinge it is so louse and light.
> The sounde borde crasede forsith the instrumente
> Throw mysgovernaunce to make notes whiche was not his intente.

After this there are numerous references to it in the inventories of country houses and the wills of the nobility and gentry. In the inventories of such families as the Manners of Belvoir and Haddon, the Sidneys of Penshurst, and the Kytsons of Hengrave Hall, there are many entries which testify to the great esteem in which music was held and to the expensive materials that were used unsparingly for the adornment of their instruments. As early as January 1525 the expenses of the Earl of Rutland [4] include:

---

[1] This is the earliest known use of the word (1511).

[2] Praetorius says in his *Theatrum instrumentorum*, 1620: " in Engelland werden alle solche Instrumenta sie sein klein oder gross, Virginal genenet."

[3] The house formerly belonged to the Percys. A manuscript copy of the proverbs is in the British Museum (Kings MS., 18, D. xi).

[4] Hist. MSS. Commission. *The manuscripts . . . preserved at Belvoir Castle*, iv, 266, 1905.

Item payde be my Lorde's comaundement for the residewe of a paire of virgynals [1] bought at my Lorde Mountjoye's, iijs. iiijd.

At Kenilworth [2] Robert Dudley, Earl of Leicester, had in 1583

an instrumente of Organs, regalles, and virginalles covered withe crimson velvett and garnished withe golde lace. A faier paire of double Virginalles. A faier paire of double Virginalles, covered with blacke velvett.

The encouragement given to music in England at this time by the royal House of Tudor was not a merely inactive patronage. Henry VIII " exercised himself dailie in . . . plaieing at the recorders, flute, virginals, in setting of songs and making of ballades," and he employed a virginalist, John Heywood, at his court. His daughters were equally accomplished and versatile, and a testimony to Elizabeth's skill on the virginals has been preserved not only in the instrument traditionally stated to have belonged to her (Pl. XIX), but in the well-known episode related by Sir James Melville,[3] who acted as ambassador between her and Mary, Queen of Scots. His post demanded a display of consummate tact, especially when Elizabeth demanded whether she or Mary excelled in beauty, stature, and other womanly qualities:

Then she asked what kind of exercises she used. I answered, that when I received my dispatch, the Queen was lately come from the Highland hunting: that when her more serious affairs permitted, she was taken up with reading of histories: that sometimes she recreated herself in playing upon the lute and virginals. She asked if she played well. I said, reasonably for a Queen. That same day after dinner my lord of Hunsdean drew me up to a quiet gallery, that I might hear some musick, (but he said that he durst not avow it) where I might hear the Queen play upon the virginals. After I had hearkened awhile, I took by the tapestry that hung before the

---

[1] The phrase " a pair of virginals "—by which the instrument was almost invariably described in England—was copied from the earlier phrase " a pair of organs." The use of the plural, Galpin (p. 226) tells us, was a translation of the Latin *organa*, which was always applied to the instrument to differentiate it from *organum*—the word used both for mediaeval descant and for a machine of any sort. It should be added that there are many instances of the use of the word " pair " to denote a set of separate things or parts forming a collective whole, *e.g.* a pair of steps, or a pair of drawers, which is still common parlance for a chest of drawers in the north of England.

[2] Hist. MSS. Commission. *Report on the manuscripts of Lord De Lisle and Dudley, preserved at Penshurst Place*, i, 491, 1925.

[3] *Memoirs*, p. 99. London, 1752.

door, I entred within the chamber, and stood a pretty space hearing her play excellently well.   But she left off immediately, so soon as she turned her about and saw me.   She appeared to be surprised to see me, and came forward, seeming to strike me with her hand; alledging she used not to play before men, but when she was solitary, to shun melancholy.   She asked how I came there.   I answered, As I was walking with my lord of Hunsdean, as we passed by the chamber-door, I heard such melody as ravished me, whereby I was drawn in ere I knew how. . . . She enquired whether my Queen or she played best.   In that I found myself obliged to give her the praise.

This brief but brilliant period at the close of the sixteenth and the beginning of the seventeenth century was the hey-day of English music, when it was most intimately bound up with the life of the people.   The fame of English virginal music is rightly everlasting, for it was composed at one of the pinnacles in our history when every domestic hearth was the scene of musical performance of a very high standard; and the people who played it made one of the essential criteria of a true education the ability to take a part in a madrigal or to play at sight a difficult [1] passage of instrumental music. During this early period the tone produced by the virginals was thin and feeble and incapable of being sustained and intensified, so that composers had recourse to various devices to add interest to their music, *e.g.* most intricate ornaments, and elaborate variations [2] on an original theme.   In the seventeenth century various attempts were made to overcome this inability to produce variety of tone: spinets were made in Italy and elsewhere in three sizes which respectively were pitched at the usual eight-foot tone, a fifth higher, and a whole octave higher (Pl. XXII); stops were added to produce a change of timbre; and pedals [3] were introduced.

All these tentative experiments were consummated in the craftsmanship of one famous family, the Ruckers of Antwerp, who made instruments that were coveted by players in every country.   Their history has been related [4] at length, but the salient facts of it are essential for an understanding of the influence they exercised over subsequent instrument-makers.   Hans the

[1] In virginal music we see the beginnings of the virtuosity which reached its apogee in the eighteenth century.

[2] For instance, Byrd's *Carman's Whistle*.

[3] The description in Mace's *Musick's Monument* of the pedal harpsichord invented by John Hayward is quoted on Pl. XL.

[4] Hipkins, pp. 80-90, and Grove, article *Ruckers*, which contains a *catalogue raisonné* of the surviving instruments made by this family.

elder and two of his four sons, Hans [1] and Andreas, are the important members of the family, and their known dated work falls between the years 1581 and 1651—a period which coincides exactly with the *haute époque* of Dutch painting. Indeed, they were in intimate association with the painters, inasmuch as they themselves were members of the artists' Guild of St. Luke, and also employed artists of high repute to decorate the lids of their instruments [2] (Pl. XXXVII). The soundboards were also usually painted with fruits, flowers, birds, and insects in a manner reminiscent of the later Flemish illuminated manuscripts (Pls. XXVI and XLII). The spirit of experiment which always accompanies the greatest period of any art is here present, for no two of their instruments are exactly alike. They had that intuitive faculty of the true craftsman which appears a little later in the Italian violin-makers of Cremona. They made both virginals (Pl. XXV) and harpsichords, and also a few double virginals. These must not be confused with the harpsichord which, we have suggested, was described by contemporary writers at that period as " a pair of double virginals." The name *double virginal* is reserved to-day for those very rare instruments which have an octave instrument fitted into the case at the side of the keyboard (Pl. XXVI). The smaller instrument [3] could be withdrawn and placed on a table, to be played by a second performer. The scarcity of these instruments is perhaps accounted for by the fact that Hans Ruckers was—if not the inventor of the octave stop—the first to incorporate it in the harpsichord as a general rule, thus removing the necessity for the small octave instruments. Other constructional improvements attributed to him are mostly connected with the harpsichord and will be discussed in the next chapter. The compass of the Ruckers' virginals was apparently three octaves and a sixth E—C, but by a device known as *short octave* it was extended to four octaves C—C. The details of this device must be mentioned here as it was generally used on all keyboard instruments in the sixteenth and early seventeenth centuries.

[1] His instruments are distinguished from those of his father by the ornamental rose in the sound-board, which has the initials I.R. (see Pl. XXIII). To avoid confusion he is usually known as Jean Ruckers.

[2] Many instruments have unfortunately been broken up on account of the high quality of their lid-paintings. The Ruckers also decorated their instruments with a yellow paper block-printed with a conventional arabesque design in black (Pl. XXV). Three different designs were used on these papers.

[3] The existence of a small octave virginal by Hans Ruckers the elder in the Leipzig University collection (Kinsky, p. 61) shows that these were sometimes made as individual instruments.

In the old music a complete diatonic scale in the lowest octave was considered essential as a basis for the melody, and at the same time economy of space on the keyboard was an urgent matter. By substituting diatonic naturals for the chromatic sharps both demands were met. There were various arrangements of the notes in the last octave to effect this but those most often used during the sixteenth and seventeenth centuries were as follows: either, the keys which apparently gave

$$F^{\sharp}\ G^{\sharp} \qquad\qquad\qquad D\ E$$
$$E\ F\ G\ A \text{ actually sounded } C\ F\ G\ A$$
$$C^{\sharp}\ D^{\sharp} \qquad\qquad\qquad A\ B$$

or those representing B C D E actually sounded G C D E.

The sharp notes thus sacrificed were not badly missed, for most music before the introduction of equal temperament in the eighteenth century was written in the major keys of F and C or the minor keys of D and G.[1]

The gradual increase in the compass of all keyboard instruments at this period must be noticed. The compass of three octaves and a major third of the virginal described by Virdung was extended a fourth lower about 1580, and again not long afterwards by another minor third making a total of four octaves—the compass of the Ruckers' virginals. Soon after the publication in 1611 of *Parthenia* (Pl. XXIV), the first printed collection of English virginal music, a minor third was added to the treble, and the compass of some instruments, including the harpsichords made by the Ruckers, was as much as four octaves and a fourth.

We must return to our main theme, the instruments themselves. In England, where virginal music was developed under the courts of Elizabeth and James I to a far higher standard than anywhere on the Continent, the word *virginal* was, we repeat, used as a generic term for all the jack instruments until about 1630. It was then confined to the rectangular coffer-like instruments with domed lids (Pl. XXVIII) of which only a dozen [2] have survived; these are English virginals proper. They show distinct traces of Flemish influence in their proportions and constructional details, and it is not unlikely that the foundations of virginal-making in England were laid by the Flemings. Contact between the two countries was encouraged by the friendly relations under Elizabeth and by the subsequent influx of Flemish craftsmen

[1] See Grove, article *Spinet*, for a fuller discussion of this subject.

[2] In Grove, article *Virginal*, they are fully described. We must notice that the period covered by their manufacture is only just over thirty years, 1641-1675.

as a result of the Spanish persecutions. Indeed we have records of the activity of these fugitive craftsmen in London.[1] In 1568 there resided in the parish of St. Martin's Le Grand " Lodewyke Tyves [*sic*], Virginall-maker, a Dutchman, and Faudevell his servant." This is none other than Ludovic Theewes the maker of the once very fine claviorganum now in the Victoria and Albert Museum (Pl. XXXVI). Again, several entries relate to William Treasurer, who is described as being in 1571 " householder of Christ Church Parish, and a denizen, maker and tuner of the Queen's Majestyes instruments; came into this realm with Sir John Walloppe about fifty years past. Jasper Blackard his servant came five years past." By 1582 the servant had also become a virginal-maker under the name Blanckart. Treasurer is also described as an organ-maker and a virginal-maker; and it is known that he made regals—the small positive organs with metal reed stops which were very popular in the sixteenth century. They were often made to fold up and resemble a book.[2]

English virginals must have been made in great numbers, for their ubiquity is noticed by Pepys in his description of the Great Fire in 1666, where he says:

> River full of lighters and boats taking in goods, and good goods on the water, and only I observed that hardly one lighter or boat in three that had the goods of a house in, but there was a pair of Virginalls in it.

The great scarceness of these instruments to-day seems less remarkable when we recall the parallel destruction of harpsichords which was ruthlessly carried out at the end of the eighteenth century owing to the increase in popularity of the piano, for there was a similar holocaust in the seventeenth century. First there was the condemnation of music and the destruction of its instruments, especially church organs, under the Commonwealth, and then there was a profound change in musical taste at the Restoration which was also reflected in the instruments. The cultivation of French music at the English court by the expert hedonist Charles II was accompanied by the introduction of the graceful *espinette* from the brilliant court of Louis XIV, which was now the centre of musical activity in Europe. An admirable illustration of this change is afforded by a few entries in the diary of that accomplished musician Pepys, whose musical observations are always

[1] *Returns of aliens dwelling in the city and suburbs of London, from the reign of Henry VIII to that of James I*, 4 vols., 1900-08. (Publications of the Huguenot Society of London.)

[2] See Galpin, p. 230.

reliable. In 1661 he is not familiar with the new name and it is still a virginal:

> I sent to my house by my Lord's desire his shippe and triangle Virginal.[1]

In 1668 he contemplates buying one of the new instruments, and he uses the right word:

> To White Hall, took Aldgate Street in my way, and there called upon one Haward [2] that makes Virginalls, and did there like of a little espinette, and will have him finish it for me; for I had a mind to a small Harpsichon,[3] but this takes up less room and will do my business as to finding out of chords and I am very well pleased that I have found it.

Later in the same year he buys another, again from Haward, and he says " cost me £5." The use of the word *triangle* by Pepys refers to the shape of the English spinet which was different from the Italian and French instruments. The keyboard is not on the longest straight side, and the charm of its form is enhanced by the graceful inward curve of one of its shorter sides. The wrest-pins are immediately above the keys.

The English spinet can be divided into three distinct chronological groups. The first covers approximately the years between 1660 and 1680: oak is used almost invariably for cases and stands (Pl. XXIX) which are un-ornamented except for occasional strap-hinges. In the second group (*circa* 1680-1715) walnut is chiefly used and sometimes the nameboard is inlaid with marquetry (Pl. XXX). Other eminent makers, in addition to Charles Haward, were Stephen Keene,[4] Charles Brackley, and Thomas and John Hitchcock. Hitherto there have been no definite biographical details about

---

[1] He often calls it simply a triangle: and he buys a " frame," *i.e.* a stand, and a " rest " for tuning it, *i.e.* a tuning hammer (Pl. XLI).

[2] Charles Haward was one of a famous family of instrument-makers (see appendix). He kept Charles II's keyboard instruments in repair: " To Mr. Charles Hayward for mending the harpsichords and pedalls in the Great Hall in the Privy Lodgings and for the private musick, for 2 whole years . . . £6 10. 0 " (De Lafontaine, p. 299).

[3] Harpsicon and Harpsical are common variations of Harpsichord. *Cf.* Claricon and Claricol for Clavichord.

[4] An advertisement in the sixth edition of John Playford's popular *Introduction to the Skill of Music* (1672) announces that " Mr. Stephen Keen, Maker of Harpsycons and Virginals, dwelleth now in Threadneedle Street at the sign of the Virginal, who maketh them exactly good, both for sound and substance." Mr. N. Lloyd has a fine spinet on its original stand and one of his virginals is owned by Mr. H. C. Moffat at Goodrich Court.

the two last-mentioned famous craftsmen, so in view of their unquestionable eminence some recently discovered records of them are related in detail.

It is perhaps the style of their instruments, as compared with other pieces of furniture, that has been responsible for the persistently erroneous attribution of all their work to the last half of the seventeenth and the early years of the eighteenth century. This is proved to be too early by the discovery of their names in the records of the Company of Haberdashers, of which they were both members. Thomas was admitted by patrimony in 1715; while John, who was almost certainly his son, was similarly admitted in 1750. They could have been admitted in any year after obtaining their majority, and Thomas's signature on the key of an instrument dated 1703 [1] suggests that some years elapsed before his admission. John likewise is found in the list of subscribers to a work by Boyce, which was printed by Walsh in 1743. The date of Thomas's death is not known, but John died in 1774.[2] They also made harpsichords, numbering all their instruments instead of dating them (Pl. XLIV). They also introduced the hitherto unprecedented compass of five octaves, always G—G, and the fact that their keyboards are chromatic throughout is another proof that they were pioneers, for it means that they were aware of the experiments being made at this time for the introduction of equal temperament and the complete chromatic scale. The tendency towards complete chromaticism was responsible for a short octave arrangement which was peculiar to a period of over sixty years from about 1660 to 1725. Whereas the last two sharps in the short octave system already described filled in the naturals of the diatonic scale, they were now each divided across into two halves: the back half gave the semitone and the front half the usual diatonic note. For instance, the last six bass notes of the spinet figured in Plate XXIX are apparently

$$\begin{array}{cccc} & \dfrac{C^{\sharp}}{C^{\sharp}} & \dfrac{D^{\sharp}}{D^{\sharp}} & \\ B & C & D & E \end{array}$$

[1] A similar signature on a spinet by Blunt dated 1664 either must be a forgery or must signify the existence of a second and older Thomas Hitchcock.

[2] The *General Evening Post* contains the following announcement: " On the 23rd Nov. 1774 died Mr. Hitchcock, organ builder in Fetter Lane, and one of the Common Councilmen for Faringdon Without." A watch-rate book shows that he lived at 28 Fetter Lane.

but the actual notes played would be

$$\frac{C^\sharp}{A} \qquad \frac{D^\sharp}{B}$$

G   C   D   E.

Instruments of the second and third quarters of the eighteenth century, which constitute the third group, show the gradual increase in the size of the spinet (Pl. XXXII), which was doubtless due to the general use of the harpsichord at this time. Those who could not afford or had not room for a harpsichord would buy a spinet, but although they were being made as late as 1785 [1] they were by that time almost obsolete. Does not Lady Teazle object to being stuck down to an " old spinet " to strum her father to sleep after a fox chase? Apart from these considerations of cost and size—to which may be added its undoubted charm as a piece of furniture—the spinet is essentially the inferior instrument, for its tone is often harsh and inevitably monotonous owing to the lack of stops. It was, therefore, naturally ousted both by the harpsichord and by the small square pianos which at this time were becoming very popular.

[1] A catalogue for the year 1782 of musical publications printed and instruments sold and let out by Longman & Broderip includes " Harpsichords, Spinets, Piano Fortes." Various other wares that would be found in a music-shop of the time are also advertised, *e.g.* " crow and raven quills, harpsicord and spinnet hammers, etc." The hammer is the tuning-hammer needed by every harpsichordist. Crow-quills for the plectra cost 10*s.* 6*d.* per 1000.

CHAPTER FOUR

THE HARPSICHORD

IT has already been suggested that the earliest form of keyboard instrument with plucked strings was not the oblong virginal or the polygonal spinet but an instrument with the keys at a right angle to the longest side, and with a "tail" like the modern grand piano: in fact instruments of this type are indicated in the earliest representations [1] (Pl. XI), and the earliest reference, which is, as in the case of the clavichord, Cersne's rules for the Minnesingers dated 1404. It is here called the *clavicymbalum*. In Italy it was the *clavicembalo*—a name which was always used for it in preference to *arpicordo*, from which the English word harpsichord is derived. In England, however, it was sometimes called the clavicymbal until the beginning of the sixteenth century, when the generic term " virginals " was more often used until the end of the seventeenth century. The earliest reference to it as the clavicymbal in England is dated 1492: it is also included in a passage in Stephen Hawes's *Passetyme of Pleasure*, 1506. This is worth quoting, as it gives us a catalogue of the instruments used at that date:

> There sat dame Musyke with all her mynstrasy;
> As tabours trumpettes with pipes melodious,
> Sakbuttes, organs, and the recorder swetely,
> Harpes, lutes, and crouddes ryght delycyous:
> Cymphans, doussemers, wyth claricimbales gloryous
> Rebeckes, clarycordes, eche in theyr degre,
> Did sytte aboute theyr ladyes mageste.

In Germany and Flanders it took from its shape the names *Kielflügel* (usually abbreviated to *Flügel* [2]) and *Staartstuk* respectively, although the Flemish

---

[1] Of an equally early date is a description of the construction of the harpsichord with a drawing which is reproduced by Gastoué (p. 113) from a ms. in the Bibliothèque Nationale (MS. Lat. 7295). Other early representations are to be found on a carving in the roof of Manchester Cathedral (figured in Galpin, fig. 21), and on an altar at Lichtenthal, painted by Hans Baldung Grien in 1496 (reproduced in the *Jahrbuch für Kunstwissenschaft*, 1923, Pl. 83).

[2] *Cembalo*, abbreviated from *clavicembalo*, was also frequently used especially in Germany.

word *clavisimbel* was used as a generic like " virginals." In France it was the *clavecin*. Its history is obscure until the sixteenth century, when the beginnings of keyboard music in Italy were accompanied by the making of harpsichords of the high quality of craftsmanship found in the earliest known *clavicembalo*, which is dated 1521 (Pl. XXXIV). These early Italian harpsichords, of which several survive,[1] were often elaborately decorated (Pl. XXXV) and were usually made of cypress wood—as opposed to the pinewood of which the Flemish instruments were always made—and they were certainly imported to England, for in the inventory of Henry VIII's musical instruments [2] there are " twoo faire paire of newe long Virginalles made harpe fasshion of Cipres." There can be little doubt that these were harpsichords, for in the diary of Marin Sanuto, under the date 6th June 1515, there is a communication [3] from Nicolo Sagudino, secretary of the Venetian ambassador at the court of Henry VIII, in which we are told that

> After dinner they [the ambassadors] were taken into rooms containing a number of organs, harpsichords, flutes, and other musical instruments.

The word used for " harpsichords " in the original diary is *clavicimbani*—a common corruption of *clavicembali*. The use of the word " virginals " in the inventory is in accordance with the custom of this period when all the domestic instruments with plucked strings went by this name. Again, the instrument described in the following extract from the same king's Privy Purse expenses [4] must have been a harpsichord:

> April, 1530. Item the vj daye paied to William Lewes for ij payer of virginalles in one coffer with iiij stoppes brought to Grenewiche iij *li*.

It is not unreasonable to interpret this as a harpsichord with two keyboards and four stops and in view of the conservative attitude of the Italian makers towards the addition of stops, it was probably of Netherlandish origin. While, therefore, the rectangular virginals and the pentagonal Italian spinets, with their one string to each note, were probably in commoner use in the sixteenth century, there is no doubt that at the beginning of the

---

[1] In addition to the Roman instrument of 1521, there is one dated 1531 by Alessandro Trasuntini in the Donaldson collection at the Royal College of Music (figured in Grove, ii, frontispiece). Another by Domenico di Pesaro, dated 1533, is figured in Kinsky, p. 88.

[2] Harleian ms. 1419 (British Museum), quoted in full by Galpin (Appendix 4).

[3] *Calendar of State Papers and Manuscripts . . . Venice. Vol. II. 1509-1519.* 1867.

[4] Sir N. H. Nicolas, *The privy purse expences of King Henry the Eighth.* London, 1827.

seventeenth century various circumstances contributed towards an increase in popularity of the larger and more powerful harpsichord, in which there were first two, and then three or sometimes four strings to each note. Not least in importance was its obvious suitability for the accompaniment from a figured bass of the recitative which was a feature of the music of Cavalieri, Peri, and the other monodists,[1] who were busy with the resuscitation of the musical declamation of Greek tragedy. The first actual performances of these beginnings of operatic form in Italy were Peri's *Euridice* in 1600, and Monteverdi's *Orfeo*, which was produced at Mantua in 1607. In both these productions harpsichords were used. In England the beginnings of opera appeared at exactly the same date, but they sprang from a different source— the dramatic entertainments known as masques,[2] which were so popular at the courts of James I and Charles I. In the text of the masque there is often a detailed description of the band, *e.g.* in Thomas Campion's famous *Discription of a Maske presented before the Kinges Maiestie at White-Hall, on Twelfth Night last in honour of Lord Hayes and his Bride*, published in 1607; it consists of

> ten Musitions, with Basse and Meane Lutes a Bandora, a double Sack-bott and an Harpsichord [3] with two treble Violins.

The making of harpsichords, as well as the less powerful virginals, at this period is always associated with the Ruckers family of Antwerp, whose activities have already been described. There can be no doubt that they were considered pre-eminent in their craft by contemporary musicians, and when Charles I required a keyboard instrument it was considered that nothing but a Ruckers harpsichord would suffice. His resident agent at Brussels, the painter Balthazar Gerbier, was commissioned to buy one, and he writes in January $163\frac{7}{8}$ to Sir Francis Windebank, Secretary of State [4]:

> The Virginall I do pitch upon is an excellent peece, made by **Johannes Rickarts att Antwerp**. Its a dobbel staert stick as called, hath foure

---

[1] Their figured basses, which appeared in 1600, were probably suggested by a study of the work of Viadana who, in 1602, popularized the thorough-bass by the publication of his famous work on the subject. In addition to the harpsichord, enlarged lutes and viols specially constructed for the purpose were also used for the *continuo*.

[2] The masque was of Italian origin and came to England from France.

[3] This is the earliest use of the word in England that I have discovered. The oldest English harpsichord in existence is dated 1622 (Pl. XL).

[4] W. N. Sainsbury, *Original unpublished papers illustrative of the life of Sir P. P. Rubens*, pp. 208 *ff.*, 1859.

registers, the place to play on att the ende.[1] The Virginal was made for the latte Infante, hath a faire picture on the inne side of the Covering, representing the Infantas parke, and on the opening, att the part were played, a picture of Rubens, representing Cupid and Psiche, the partie asks £30 starling. Those Virginals which have noe pictures cost £15.

Secretary Windebank replies that he does not much respect the accessories of ornament or paintings, and that he would rather choose " a very good one plaine and without these curiosities." However, the one originally chosen by Gerbier is sent:

" but," writes the Secretary, " the workman that made it, was much mistaken in it, and it wantes 6 or 7 Keyes, so that it is utterly unserviceable. If either he could alter it, or wolde change it for another that may have more Keyes, it were well: but as it is, our music is marr'd." [2]

Gerbier answers that he will sell it for what he can get and have another made by Ruckers " the best master here," who, however, with the indifference found in the successful trader, retorts that " this Virginall cannot be altered, and none else made on sale." Several constructional improvements have always been attributed to Hans the elder, *e.g.* the addition of the octave strings, the double keyboard, and the abolition of short octave for a completely chromatic keyboard. But octave strings have been found in earlier Italian *clavicembali*, and the instrument belonging to Henry VIII probably had two keyboards.[3] It is now also recognized that these improvements are to be found on the earlier *claviorganum* or organ-harpsichord (Pl. **XXXVI**), which

[1] Clearly it was a two-manual harpsichord (*staartstuk*).

[2] This protest was occasioned by a constructional feature of the Ruckers instruments which was abolished about 1650, and is therefore very obscure; but Hipkins (p. 87) discovered an unaltered harpsichord by Jean Ruckers of exactly the same date as Windebank's letter (1638), which explains the missing keys. The upper keyboard had a compass of three octaves and a semitone, B-C, but the lower one had one of four octaves and a semitone, E-F, which was extended by " short octave " to four octaves and a fourth, C-F. The lower manual, however, was strung so that the notes were a fourth lower than the keys actually signified; and the top F was thus the same as the top C on the upper keyboard. The gap made by the missing notes in the upper manual was filled by a wooden block. This arrangement was designed to facilitate the transposing of the old church modes to the level of the singer's voice. It was doubtless an instrument of this type that Jean Ruckers supplied to Gerbier.

[3] A clavicytherium, or upright harpsichord, of the first half of the sixteenth century has two keyboards (see p. 113).

had a greater popularity than is usually credited to it.[1]   However, what had
been but tentative experiments in the past, he now made the general practice,
and he fixed a standard for all future makers to follow.   Of almost equal
fame was Jean Ruckers' nephew, Jean Couchet (Pl. LIV), who first worked
with his uncle for sixteen years.   He is now known to have limited the octave
register to the lower keyboard and to have added a second unison string of
ordinary eight-foot tone " which has a rather sharper quality than the other
one, which also causes an agreeable sweetness by reason of this being rather
more than a straw's breadth longer than the other." [2]   This enabled the
player to use the keyboards in contrast one with the other, the upper for soft
passages with one unison string, the lower for loud passages with both
unison strings and the octave.   The great importance of these improvements
is summed up by Hipkins in these words:

> he changed the double keyboard harpsichord from a mere transposing
> instrument, contrived to accommodate the authentic and plagal church
> modes with the singer's capabilities, to a forte and piano instrument.

This supremacy of the Netherlandish instrument-makers at the close of
the sixteenth century is, we have seen, contemporary with the supremacy of
English composers whose creation of the keyboard style is one of the land-
marks in our musical past.   Both, however, now fell from their high estate;
the one with the decline of Antwerp as a centre of culture and commerce,
and the other with the growth of Puritanism, which culminated in 1644 in
an order to strip the churches of their organs.[3]   Germany, torn by religious
wars, produced little but choral music, and the seeds of vocal music sown in

---

[1] The earliest record of these instruments is dated 1480 (see Van der Straeten, vii,
248 *ff.*), and they were made as late as the second half of the eighteenth century, when
square pianos were also combined with a small positive organ.

[2] Hipkins quotes this (p. 83) from the very interesting correspondence between Con-
stantin Huygens, secretary to the Prince of Orange and an accomplished amateur of music,
and G. F. Duarte, a rich dealer in precious stones in Antwerp, also an enthusiastic musician.
A selection from Huygens' correspondence, relating to music, etc., has been published (see
the Bibliography), and it throws much light on the state of music in Europe in the seventeenth century.

[3] Hawkins remarks that most organ-makers sought employment elsewhere cabinet-
making, but craftsmen of such repute as Loosemoore of Exeter, Preston of York, Thamer of
Peterborough, and the brothers Dallam, seem to have continued their trade.   Loosemoore,
we know, turned his hand to virginals (Pl. XXVIII), and Thamer is mentioned in the
steward's accounts at Haddon Hall as having received £7 in 1648 for " repareing and setting
in order both the Orgaines and Harpsicall."

Italy at the beginning of the century had grown into an overblown monstrosity. France, however, was unquestionably the first state in Europe, both in arms and arts; and it was here that instrumental music now received the most devoted attention, both of theorists [1] and performers, at the glittering court of Louis Quatorze. Composition for the harpsichord was here treated seriously and a school of *clavecinistes* arose amongst whom Couperin [2] and Rameau were notable figures.

We have already seen that English music at the Restoration was completely frenchified, and that as a result the spinet enjoyed great popularity: but the harpsichord with its larger tone was gradually increasing in importance with the beginnings of the public performance of music. [3] It was also used in the orchestra by the conductor, who was often the composer, for filling in the harmony. The leader of the first violins sometimes disputed the authority of the conductor as he presided at the harpsichord, and we read of quarrels between the two. Towards the end of the seventeenth century, then, we find that the well-known spinet-makers such as Keene and the elder Hitchcock are also making the harpsichord (Pl. XLIV); and with the arrival of the eighteenth century it became the standard keyboard instrument, its position being comparable with that occupied by the grand pianoforte to-day. The pattern adopted by the Ruckers was still followed, and the traditions of their *atelier* were brought by a Fleming called Tabel direct to England, [4] whose turn it now was to produce the finest instruments.

We must, however, notice in passing that attempts were made to popularize an upright harpsichord. [5] The idea was not new, for in several

[1] There had been many important additions to the literature of music in the first half of the century, *e.g.* the works of Cerone, Praetorius, Mersenne (Pl. XLI), Kircher, etc. See the Bibliography for titles.

[2] His famous " method "—*L'art de toucher le clavecin*—was published in 1716. The influence of this work on other composers, especially Bach, is an interesting study. It is clearly reflected in the execution of the *agrémens* (ornaments) and in the dance forms and suites used by Bach.

[3] Concerts were first held in about 1672 under the direction of John Banister, who was for a time leader of Charles II's " violins ": and in 1678 Thomas Britton, the musical small-coal man, started his weekly concerts at which—at a later date—Handel performed on a chamber-organ and Pepusch played the harpsichord.

[4] " Broadwood, writing in 1838, gives us the important information that Tabel had learned his business in the house of the successor of the Ruckers of Antwerp " (Dale, p. 21).

[5] A notice in the press in 1726 informs " all Gentlemen and Ladies, lovers of Art and Harmony, there is lately finished a Harpsichord which stands upright in an uniform Case and is a most elegant piece of Furniture contrived to stand in less room than a small Scrutore. To be seen at the Inventor's Mr. Thomas Barton, etc." Samuel Blumer also made them.

of the musical treatises of the sixteenth and seventeenth centuries there are descriptions and rude woodcuts of a harpsichord stood on end with the " tail " pointing upwards, to which the name *clavicytherium* was given. It was, like the upright piano, obviously intended to save space. Virdung (1511) describes it as being newly invented and having strings of gut, but both his description and his illustration of it are deplorably inadequate. The woodcut is the wrong way round, as are those of the virginal and clavichord, the engraver having forgotten to reverse the drawings. A century later it is described by Praetorius and Mersenne. The latter, after telling us in his *Harmonicorum Libri XII* that it originated and was very popular in Italy, suggests with characteristic gravity that it should be placed in such a way as to allow the wind blowing through the window to strike the strings and thus to increase the tone! A most interesting specimen dating from the end of the fifteenth century has survived (Pl. XXXIII). The only other deviation from the usual methods of construction which was seriously contemplated was provoked by an attempt to overcome the brief duration of tone—an inevitable accompaniment of the plucked string. The production of a sustained tone had constantly been attempted, and more than once the invention of an instrument on the principle of the hurdy-gurdy is recorded.[1] Even Bach considered the removal of this serious limitation:

> To remedy at least one main defect in the harpsichord—namely, its brief resonance—in the year 1740 (or thereabout) he devised a " Lauten-clavicymbel " [2] (Lute-harpsichord), which was constructed by the organ-builder Zacharias Hildebrand, under his direction; the greater duration of tone was produced by gut strings, of which it had two to each note, and these were supplemented by a set of metal strings giving a four-foot tone. When the ringing tone of these was checked by a damper of cloth the

---

[1] In the *Nürmbergisch Geigenwerck* of about 1620 (Pl. XXXVIII) the keys brought the strings into contact with several wheels covered with rosined parchment which were rotated by a foot-treadle. A Spanish instrument of this type is in the Museum at Brussels (Pl. XXXIX). The instrument mentioned by Pepys in his diary on 5th October 1664, under the name "Arched Viall " was evidently another attempt to make a mechanical chest of viols in which wheels replaced the bows and the stopping was done by means of the keyboard. He saw it at a meeting of the Royal Society. Evelyn, a member of the Society, also saw it and described it as " a harpsichord with gut strings . . . made vocal by a wheel and zone of parchment that rubbed horizontally against the strings." See also Grove, article *Sostinente Pianoforte*.

[2] Two of these instruments are mentioned in the inventory of Bach's effects and musical instruments. See C. S. Terry, *Bach. A biography*, p. 271, 1928.

instrument sounded much like a real lute, while without this it had more of the gloomy character of the theorbo. In size it was shorter than the ordinary harpsichord.[1]

In the following year, 1741, an English craftsman, Roger Plenius, took out a patent for a harpsichord with gut strings, which he called the Lyrichord. In an advertisement from the *London Evening Post* for 14th February 1747, the maker

> Humbly gives Notice to all Gentlemen and Ladies, that his LYRICHORD which imitates the Violin, Violoncello, Double Bass, and Organ, by Catgut Strings alone, and never goes out of Tune, is now, after two Years Recess reviv'd, with great Improvements, and will be exhibited to publick View, Next Thursday, from Twelve at Noon till Four o' Clock, and so to continue every Day Sundays excepted.

Wheels were used instead of quills and the strings were to be kept constantly in tune by a system of weights and pulleys. It is not known whether this was an independent idea or whether he had heard of Bach's instrument: but it is certain that neither of these experiments had any important effect on the subsequent manufacture of keyboard instruments.

The ordinary standard English harpsichord of the eighteenth century was, we repeat, universally acknowledged as the best of its kind after the Ruckers instruments; but we must observe that all branches of music in England at this time—composition, performance, and the construction of instruments—were dominated by foreigners. We need not therefore be surprised that the two leading harpsichord makers, whose great repute was only equalled by the vast fortunes they amassed, were also resident aliens. They were the Swiss, Burckhardt Tschudi, and the German, Jakob Kirchmann, whose names were always anglicized into Burkat Shudi and Jacob Kirkman. Burney comments on their instruments with approval:

> I must observe, that the Germans work much better out of their own country, than they do in it, if we may judge by the harpsichords of Kirkman and Shudi; the piano fortes of Backers; and the organs of Snetzler; which far surpass, in goodness, all the keyed instruments that I met with, in my tour through Germany.

The Netherlandish instruments he regarded with disfavour:

[1] Spitta, English ed., ii, 46. Adlung also mentions this experiment.

At present there is a good workman at Antwerp, of the name of Bull,[1] who was Dulcken's apprentice, and who sells his double harpsichords for a hundred ducats each, with only plain painted cases, and without swell or pedals; the work too of Vanden Elsche,[2] a Flamand, has a considerable share of merit; but in general, the present harpsichords, made here after the Ruckers model, are thin, feeble in tone, and much inferior to those of our best makers in England.

Equal condemnation is given to the Italian instruments of this period, and the three English harpsichords which he discovered on his tour through Italy—one by Shudi and the other two by Kirkman—were regarded by the Italians " as so many phenomena." These two men, whose pre-eminence was so securely established by contemporary opinion, carried on the Flemish traditions, for they were both employed by Tabel. Whereas we scarcely know anything about Tabel,[3] the lives of his two foremen, as Burney calls them, are comparatively familiar to musical historians.[4] Although Kirkman stole a march on his rival by marrying Tabel's widow in 1738, a month after the funeral, he did not carry on the business but set up independently at the King's Arms, Broad Street. Shudi had probably started his own business a few years earlier at the Plume of Feathers in Meard Street, Soho,[5] for one of his harpsichords dated 1729 has survived: it was made for the singer Anna Strada and, as Dale suggests, was probably given to her by Handel, who had brought her back from Italy to sing in his new operas. Handel was a per-

[1] One of his harpsichords, dated 1776, is in the Brussels collection (Cat. No. 1601).

[2] At Berlin there is a harpsichord by this maker dated 1710 (Cat. No. 2235).

[3] The late Countess of Radnor possessed the only harpsichord made by him that has survived. It is dated 1721, has two manuals, and in appearance resembles a Kirkman. His instruments were much prized in the eighteenth century. The following announcement from the *Evening Post* for 30th May 1723 is of interest: " Mr. Tabel, the famous Harpsichord Maker, has 3 Harpsichords to dispose of, which are and will be the last of his making, since he intends to leave off Business. At his House in Oxendon Street over agingst the Black Horse in Piccadilly. N.B. He has also some fine Airs-wood [*i.e.* harewood] for furnishing the Insides, to dispose of."

[4] W. Dale's very interesting monograph, *Tschudi the Harpsichord Maker*, gives a vivid picture of Shudi, his patrons and apprentices, and his craft; and I am indebted to it for much of the following information. It was compiled from the old books and papers belonging to Messrs. Broadwood, his business successors in a direct line of descent.

[5] Soho—especially the streets bordering on Golden Square—was a centre of the musical instrument trade throughout the eighteenth century. There was a colony of Swiss makers here at this date, *e.g.* Zopfi and Blumer (Pl. XLIX), in addition to Shudi; and Snetzler, the organ-maker, with whom Shudi collaborated in the production of organ-harpsichords (*claviorgana*).

sonal friend of Shudi and, although tradition names the Ruckers harpsichord now in the Victoria and Albert Museum (Pl. XLII) as his favourite
instrument, there can be little doubt that he used one of Shudi's instruments
as well.[1] He also gained for him the custom of his patron,[2] the Prince of Wales,
which is reflected in the sign chosen for his shop. The King, whose relations
with his son were notoriously strained, accordingly patronized Kirkman.

With an increase in business Shudi moved in 1742 to larger premises in
Great Pulteney Street, and it was for the overmantel in his new house that
the portrait of him and his family was painted (Pl. XLVIII). Here amongst
his apprentices we must notice the Scotchman John Broadwood, who, in 1769,
was rewarded for his good services in the traditional manner with the hand
of his daughter, and a partnership,[3] which was continued with young
Burkat Shudi after his father's death in 1773. Plenty of evidence of the
success with which the business was carried on is found in the list of influ-
ential customers quoted by Dale, amongst whom were included the artists
Gainsborough, Reynolds, and Bartolozzi; but the popularity of the piano
was now increasing so rapidly that in 1793 Broadwood made his last harpsichord—" a double keyed harpsichord with swell, etc., cross banded with
sattin wood. Cypher in front, etc. £84."[4] The swell was a device patented
by Shudi in 1769 [5] for giving gradation of tone: it was later transferred to
the organ and, when the patent expired, was added to older harpsichords.
Kirkman countered this by a clumsy arrangement, also worked by a pedal,
which lifted half the lid of the instrument. The swell is illustrated in the
reproduction of the fine harpsichord which Shudi made for Maria Theresa

[1] The following sale notice is taken from the *Morning Herald*: " Handel's Harpsichord,
at Mr. Cross's opposite the Town Hall, Oxford. On Thurs, the 26th June 1788, at Two
o'Clock in the afternoon. A Capital double Key'd HARPSICHORD, by BUREAT SCHUDI [*sic*],
made for the Immortal Handel and used by him till his death, at the different Concerts in
London. It consists of four stops, which are as follow: two unisons, an upper and lower
octave, has a powerful tone and is well calculated for Concerts."
[2] Handel now enjoyed the Prince's friendship in place of the organized enmity which
had lasted for many years.
[3] The first harpsichord to be signed by both is dated 1770, but some bearing Shudi's
name only were made after this date.
[4] The standard charges were 35 gns. for a single manual, 40 gns. for a single manual
with octave stop, 50 gns. for the same with a swell, and 80 gns. for a double manual with
octave and swell.
[5] Patent No. 947. He had added the swell to instruments by 1766, as it is found on the
two harpsichords he made in that year for Frederick the Great. See Dale, cap. iv. Mozart
played on one of them.

(Pl. LII), where a full description of the stops on his instruments will also be found.

Although less is known about Kirkman [1] his harpsichords were equally popular. Their tone is usually somewhat stronger and the arrangement of the stops is different (Pl. L). Burney regarded them as more durable than Shudi's, but there are no grounds for this criticism. As for other English makers the extraordinary scarcity of their instruments reflects the extent to which the supply was almost monopolized by these two firms,[2] for the greater number of harpsichord makers to be found in the Appendix to this work—although they number over sixty—cannot be commemorated by examples of their craftsmanship. Their instruments, too, were doubtless distinguished by the comfortable solidity, sound proportions, graceful lines, and restraint in ornamentation, which were noticeable characteristics of the contemporary furniture. More elaborate cases were, of course, sometimes made for distinguished patrons,[3] and the famous furniture designers of the period seem occasionally to have been employed. Sheraton designed a grand piano for Don Godoy, prime minister of Spain (Pl. LXII), and Robert Adam designed a harpsichord and a square piano for Catherine, Empress of Russia (Pl. LIII).

Harpsichords made in other countries during the eighteenth century are not without interest in spite of the superiority of the English instruments and the denunciation made by Burney of the continental craftsmen. In Italy, where attention was now concentrated on the violin, keyboard music was at a discount with the notable exception of Domenico Scarlatti's harpsichord music which, however, was not appreciated in his own country. But we must notice the appearance in this country, and elsewhere, of harpsichords

[1] See Grove. He died worth £200,000, probably in 1778, and was succeeded by his nephew Abraham, whom he had taken into partnership in 1773. Both their names continued to be inscribed on instruments until 1789, when Abraham was joined by his son Joseph. From 1798 the firm was directed by Joseph alone.

[2] Dealers and less well-known makers evidently passed off inferior instruments as being made by them. Mr. Arthur Hill has a parchment dated 1771 on which are the pleadings in an action brought by Jacob Kirkman against " Robert Ffalknor " (perhaps the Faulkner in the Appendix) who " exposed to sale a certain Harpsichord for a large sum of money to wit the Sum of 27*l.* 6*s.* as and for a Harpsichord made by the said Jacob." Jacob claimed £500 damages being " greatly hurt and injured and damnified in his good Name, fame, and credit," but it is not known whether he won his suit. This practice is also suggested by advertisements in the press, *e.g.* " Harpsichords to be sold cheap, among which is a real Kirkman's."

[3] *E.g.* the harpsichords made by Shudi for Frederick the Great (figured in Dale, pp. 42 *ff.*), and a few harpsichords made by Kirkman (Pl. L).

with three manuals (Pls. **XLV** and **LI**), which dispensed thereby with the use of stops.   Grave doubts, however, have been expressed of the authenticity of some of the surviving examples.

In France, its sparkling tone and its possibilities for the artist-decorator made it essentially the instrument of the *salon*.   Here, especially, the Ruckers' instruments continued to be used.   They were first extended to a compass of five octaves—an operation with which we must associate especially the name of Pascal Taskin, who was the most renowned French harpsichord maker of the century after his master, Etienne Blanchet.[1]   Several existing instruments by the Ruckers family, and the harpsichord by Couchet figured in Pl. LIV, have inscriptions showing that they were brought up-to-date in the eighteenth century in this way.[2]   Taskin is also remembered for the reintroduction—it was called an invention at the time—of leather (*peau de buffle*) for the plectra of the jacks in place of the usual quill. The decoration of his charming *clavecin*, in the Victoria and Albert Museum (Pl. LV) reminds us that on the Continent rich ornamentation was usually lavished on the cases which make a striking contrast with the comparatively plain English harpsichords.   The most fashionable artists were employed to decorate the cases, and the choicest woods and varnishes were used.[3] The national characteristics of ingenuity and delicacy of work are also reflected in such mechanical devices as the folding harpsichord (*clavecin brisé*) invented by Marius (Pl. XLV), and the substitution of a row of foot-pedals instead of the usual hand-stops on the name-board.   The stringing differs from that of the Netherlandish and English harpsichords, inasmuch as each keyboard has an independent set of strings.   The system was also adopted in Germany where large harpsichords were occasionally made with a set of strings giving sixteen-foot tone known as the Bourdon.   These were placed above the usual two unison and octave strings and gave great

[1] Other French clavecin makers of repute were the Denis family, Antoine Valter (*fl.* 1720-55), J. Henri Hemsch (*fl.* 1747-75), F. B. Peronard (*fl.* 1760-89), and Joseph Treyer called *L'Empereur* (*fl.* 1770-89).   In France also the proportion of Swiss and German craftsmen was noticeable.

[2] The usual term to denote the abolition of the short octave and extension of the bass was *mis en ravalement*, or the word *refait*, or simply *fait*, followed by the restorer's name.

[3] Documentary evidence of this and the prices paid, is found in Bricqueville's interesting selection from the French periodical *Les Affiches, Annonces et Avis Divers*, which was founded in 1752 and published twice weekly until 1792.   The following entries are typical: " Clavecin de Rukers dont le pied est marqueterie.   Il a été fait par Boule, le père, avec des ornements dorés d'ormoulu et de belles peintures.—Très beau clavecin de Rukers peint par Watteau.—Clavecin de Rukers verni par Martin.   Prix 300 livres " (Pl. XLVII).

depth of tone. Bach had one of these instruments [1] and his use of it is reflected in some of his compositions, *e.g.* some of the *Thirty Variations* composed for his pupil Goldberg.[2] The making of harpsichords in Germany, however, was not so extensive, owing to the great popularity of the clavichord as a domestic instrument and the enthusiastic encouragement given to the development of the piano at a far earlier date than in other countries.[3]

The death-knell of the harpsichord was sounded not by the introduction of the piano, but by the change in musical taste, which resulted in the perfection of that instrument. This is not a quibble but an assertion of the principle that the invention of instruments does not create a new kind of music, but is in response to the demands of composers who are often in advance of the general taste. Professor Dent has concisely summed up this important question in these words [4]:

It is a mistaken view of history to suppose that makers of instruments preceded composers in the discovery of new possibilities. It is only the second-rate composers who are stimulated by mechanical inventions; the great composers imagine new possibilities and it is they who suggest to the instrument makers the directions in which they can improve their wares. At the beginning of the nineteenth century the pianoforte makers had little or no idea of producing the quality of tone which we now associate with this instrument. Old pianofortes often sound like harpsichords, not just because they are old, but because their makers meant them to sound like that. . . . The advantage of the pianoforte lay not in its different tone-colour, but in its power of dynamic gradation.

I cannot agree with the opinion simultaneously expressed by another writer [5] that " the characteristics and qualities of the instruments that were available have always governed the inspiration of composers. The instru-

---

[1] It is now in the Hochschule für Musik, Berlin, and is figured in Grove, Pl. xxxii. The registration is as follows: on the lower manual, one 16 ft. and one 8 ft. pitch string; on the upper, one 8 ft. and one 4 ft. pitch string.

[2] In this work we find one of the very rare examples of a composer's instructions for the use of stops. In the *Italian Concerto* he gives clear indications of a change of keyboard by the use of the abbreviations *pia* and *for*. Handel, in a small group of pieces in the Earl of Aylesford MSS., actually uses three and four staves showing the exact treatment of the two manuals.

[3] The best-known makers were Albert Hass of Hamburg and his son Hieronymus Albrecht Hass, Gottfried Silbermann of Dresden (1683-1755) and his nephew Johann Andreas Silbermann of Strasburg (1712-83).

[4] *The Dominant*, June 1928, p. 15.

[5] G. R. Hayes, *Musical instruments and their music*, p. 1.

ments came first, the music followed." It might as well be said that with the invention of chairs we learned how to sit down.

After the death of Bach and Handel music gradually shook off the gilded patronage of an emasculate aristocracy and composers sought, even at the cost of privation, for the true expression of emotion. The texture of a dry academic counterpoint gave way to the form born of pure melody, richly glowing with harmonic colour. This change was naturally accompanied by a demand for more instrumental variety and gradation of tone, and the pianoforte, at once more robust than the clavichord and more expressive than the harpsichord, was soon seen to be the instrumental vehicle for the new music. By the end of the century [1] the " grand pianoforte harpsichord "— as the piano was called for a time to modify the abruptness of the change [2]— had replaced its predecessor both for private and public performance.[3]

In concluding this chapter we must welcome the undoubted revival of the harpsichord at the present day. Not only are the few old instruments that have survived being used for the performance of eighteenth-century music, but modern instruments are being constructed in the light of modern scientific knowledge and with the benefit of greater resources for materials. It is obvious that the substitution of foot pedals for all hand stops is desirable as it allows the player—as foot couplers do the organist—to effect the changes of tone without removing the hands from the keyboard (see the frontispiece). Modern craftsmen also make these pedals with a " half-hitch ": this device, by allowing the rack of jacks to be brought on only half the full distance, and the quill-points therefore to give the strings a feebler pluck, enables a crescendo of tone to be obtained. And the modern harpsichord at least has the advantage of being comparatively reliable, whereas an old one the player must know even as he knows himself. For all its mellow beauty there are occasions when it has to be coaxed and wheedled like a petulant child.

---

[1] Engel (*Mus. Times*, 1879, 1st July) said " the late Mr. Kirkman told me that he with his father constructed the last harpsichord in the year 1809."

[2] A Covent Garden play-bill for 21st May 1793 is inscribed as follows: " Master Field, a child of nine years old, will perform a sonata from Op. 2 Clementi on one of Longman and Broderip's newly invented Grand Piano Forte Harpsichords." John Field, infant prodigy and inventor of the nocturne, was employed by Clementi as a salesman until 1804.

[3] The following entry in the accounts of the Earl of Verulam, at Gorhambury (*Hist. MSS. Comm.*, 1906, p. 209), speaks for itself: " 1794, Nov. 29.—Account of Longman and Broaderip. ' A patent pianoforte, 27*l*. 6*s*.; they gave credit for a 2nd hand harpsichord 10*l*. 10*s*.' " In the following year the King's Band used a harpsichord at the rehearsal of the Birthday Ode at St. James' Palace on 4th June, but a grand piano was sent for the performance (Dale, p. 8).

CHAPTER FIVE

THE PIANOFORTE UNTIL THE INTRODUCTION OF IRON INTO ITS FRAME IN THE
YEAR 1820

THE common statement that the piano[1] was invented in the year 1709 is apt to imply a sudden growth from non-existence to maturity rather than a gradual development to mechanical perfection; and there can be little doubt that just as the psaltery was given keys so there must have been experiments made to construct a keyed dulcimer, especially as uniformity of tone—the most serious limitation of the mechanically plucked string—could be avoided by the use of hammers on the struck string. The earliest recorded attempt to make an instrument of this kind with gradation of tone is that of an instrument maker named Paliarino, who mentions in the year 1598 what he calls a *Pian e Forte* in some correspondence with the Duke of Modena.[2] The name he gives, however, does not prove that it had a hammer action, and it may well have been a harpsichord with some device for varying the tone, or a *claviorganum*, as one of his instruments is described as having an organ underneath. Of twelve years later date is the instrument formerly in the collection of M. René Savoye of Paris which, although more a keyed dulcimer than a piano as we know it,[3] is at least evidence of an early hammer action.

There were doubtless other experiments between this date and the year 1709, when four pianos made by Bartolomeo Cristofori, harpsichord-maker

---

[1] I make no apology for using throughout this chapter this usual abbreviation. It would, however, have been more in keeping with the character of the instrument had the name *fortepiano*, which was in fact commonly used in the eighteenth century, given us *forte* as an abbreviation.

[2] The text of these letters and an inventory of the Duke's instruments were published in 1879—L. F. Valdrighi, *Musurgiana*, Modena. See Grove, article *Pianoforte* for further information.

[3] Dolmetsch describes it as follows (p. 431): "A very early pianoforte dated 1610, unquestionably genuine. . . . It is apparently of Dutch origin, and was made for a French nobleman. It has very small hammers attached to the keys, showing a simple form of the Viennese action. It has no dampers and never had any. No doubt the player occasionally stopped the vibrations of the strings with his hands, as dulcimer players do, when confusion became objectionable. The instrument altogether looks much like a large dulcimer." It had a compass of four octaves.

and keeper of the instruments to Prince Ferdinand dei Medici, were inspected by Francesco Scipione, Marchese di Maffei.   They had, perhaps, been made a few years earlier, for Cristofori had been brought by the Prince from Padua, his native town, to Florence, about 1690.   Maffei had come to seek the Prince's patronage for a literary publication entitled *Giornale dei letterati d'Italia*, and it was in this work that Cristofori's invention was first communicated to the world anonymously by Maffei [1] in 1711.   The diagram of the action which accompanies the description shows such a remarkable mechanical efficiency that, in spite of it probably being the practical fulfilment of an idea conceived many years earlier, we can allow Cristofori's self-bestowed title of *Inventor* [2] to pass unchallenged.   Three of the four instruments that Maffei saw were shaped like harpsichords and the two surviving pianos made by Cristofori are of the same shape [3]; in fact their construction in an outer protecting case with the characteristic battens, the shallowness of the cases, and their maker's name for them—*gravicembalo col piano e forte*—all proclaim them to be virtually hammer-harpsichords. [4]   They contain all the essential parts of the hammer action which form the basis of the vastly developed and —in comparison—very intricate action of our modern piano.   These are best studied with diagrams in the technical text-books, [5] but a brief and simple description of them is essential for an understanding of the development of the instrument.

The small hammers by which the strings are struck consist of a shaft, known as the shank, at one end of which is the hammer-head (*e*), covered at first with leather but now with felt, and at the other the butt (*d*)—a more solid piece through which is the axis of the hammer.   In all except the old German and Viennese actions—to be described presently—the axis is fixed and the

---

[1] Vol. v, p. 144.   Rimbault (pp. 95 *ff.*) gives a verbatim transcription of the article and an inaccurate translation.   Although Maffei wrote the name as Cristofali, inscriptions on surviving instruments and an autograph prove that Cristofori is the correct name.

[2] It must be noticed that this word was sometimes used by craftsmen to mean *Maker* without any claim to invention.

[3] One dated 1720 (Pl. LVI) is now in the Metropolitan Museum, New York, and the other, made in 1726, is at the Musikwissenschaftliches Institut, Leipzig, and is figured in Grove, Pl. xl.   The action in these is an improvement on that described by Maffei in 1711.

[4] The two strings for each note, however, are not arranged in pairs as in the harpsichord, but are equidistant, and a wedge-shaped damper falls between each pair tuned in unison.   The far greater strain imposed on the case is resisted by a stronger wrest-plank and a strip of oak for the hitch-pins which is fixed on to the soundboard.

[5] I am especially indebted to Hipkins for much of the technical information throughout this chapter.

impetus necessary to raise the hammer is conveyed from the key through the indispensable direct lever known as the hopper (*b*). This is set in the key-lever (*a*) and fits into a notch (*c*) in the butt of the hammer, or into an intermediary under-hammer (*k*). A wire spring (*i*) regulates the angle of the hopper and ensures its return to the notch—a movement which is responsible for the velocity of the hammer and that responsiveness to the player's touch which is the chief feature of the instrument. Another function of paramount importance performed by the hopper is the provision of the escapement, *i.e.* the space between the string and the hammer when raised to its fullest height without impetus. This is, of course, necessary for the

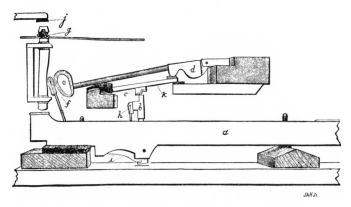

CRISTOFORI'S ACTION

free vibration of the strings, as the hammer would stifle the sound unless it could rebound a little distance after contact. In addition to the hopper the key-lever raises a spade-shaped pad (*f*) on the end of a small shaft fixed into the end farthest from the keys. This is known as the check, and its function is to catch the hammer as it falls and thus facilitate the quick repetition of the stroke by preventing the hammer from reaching its seat and having to be raised again the whole distance of its course. The only other essential part is the damper (*g*). This is a small piece of cloth which is also raised when the key is depressed, and with its release comes into contact with the string and stops the vibration. These are the absolutely necessary parts of the action of a piano whatever its shape may be and whatever degree of elaboration the mechanism may have reached.

Although Cristofori's invention seems all the more remarkable in view of these constructional details it was neither honoured nor developed in his own country,[1] but it was welcomed by the German craftsmen who, with characteristic zeal and astuteness, utilized the idea to the advantage of posterity. We can pass over the claims for the invention made in 1716 by Marius, the French harpsichord-maker, and in 1717 by Schröter the Saxon musician; the four *clavecins à maillets* of the former [2] were probably never constructed, and the two " claviers with hammers " of the latter were thoroughly impracticable.[3] It was the publication at Hamburg in 1725 of a translation of Maffei's article in the *Giornale dei letterati* that kindled the spark in Germany by attracting the attention of Gottfried Silbermann, the famous organ-builder and clavichord-maker of Dresden. After experimenting for about eight years he had made two pianofortes, shaped like harpsichords, and with Cristofori's action,[4] which he considered fit to be submitted to J. S. Bach for criticism. This the great composer readily gave—saying that the touch was too heavy and the tone of the treble strings too thin—with the result that Silbermann was dismayed into temporary inactivity. He persevered with his experiments, however, so successfully that he not only produced two instruments which satisfied Bach[5] but also received an order from Frederick the Great to supply his palaces at Potsdam with pianos. Burney saw the one made for the *Neues Palais*:

> His majesty's concert room is ornamented with glasses of an immense size, and with sculpture, partly gilt, and partly of the most beautiful green varnish, by Martin of Paris; the whole furniture and ornaments of this room are most refined and exquisite taste. There is a *piano forte* made by Silbermann of Neuberg, beautifully varnished and embellished; and a tortoise-shell desk for his majesty's use, most richly and elegantly inlaid with silver.

In the midst of this baroque extravagance " old Bach " was received by Frederick on the occasion of his well-known visit in 1747, when he played on one of these instruments.

---

[1] Ponsicchi (p. 37) tells us that he died in 1731 and the instruments he was making were completed by his pupil Ferrini, who made the piano given by the Queen of Spain to the famous *castrato* singer Farinelli.

[2] Rimbault (pp. 102 *ff.*) has reproduced the original descriptions and drawings which were published in 1735.

[3] Rimbault, pp. 109-110.

[4] Probably copied from the less satisfactory diagram of 1711 and not from an existing instrument.

[5] Bach visited Dresden in 1733 and again in 1736, and it was probably on one, or both, of these visits that he tried Silbermann's instruments.

Up till now the clavichord and harpsichord had been too firmly estab-lished in the regard of composers to be ousted by the new instrument,[1] but by about 1750 it was receiving more attention from German musicians, and craftsmen were busy with constructional experiments. One result of their efforts, which had the most far-reaching effects, was the introduction of the square (rectangular) piano. This was not entirely an independent invention: for, just as the harpsichord was the basis of the grand piano shape adopted by Cristofori and Silbermann, so the clavichord was the model for the square piano. Tradition names Friederici of Gera, a famous organ-builder, as having been the first to make one of these instruments in 1758,[2] but not one made by him in this shape has survived, and there are indications of the manufacture of square pianos—as well as the conversion of clavichords into pianos—as early as 1750.[3] These activities in Germany now received a serious check with the outbreak of the Seven Years' War in 1756, and a band of German craftsmen made their way to England, bringing with them the square piano.

The introduction of the piano to England at this comparatively late date is explained by the unassailable popularity of the English harpsichords. The only attempt made before this time to construct one in England had been a failure, if we can believe Burney's [4] story of a grand piano made in Rome by a monk, Father Wood, and bought by Fanny Burney's " daddy," Samuel Crisp of Chesington, who sold it for a hundred guineas to the dandy Fulk Greville.[5] Roger Plenius, the maker of the Lyrichord, tried to copy it but, inasmuch as it was limited to pieces of a *tempo* of the *Dead March* from *Saul*, no more was heard of it. We can, therefore, regard the arrival about 1760 of Johann Zumpe and his fellow countrymen [6] as the opening of a new chapter in the history of English music. Zumpe had been employed in Germany by Silbermann, and on his arrival in England he worked for a

---

[1] The piano does not receive an entry in Walther's lexicon (1732), but Cristofori is mentioned—under the name Cristofali—as the inventor of a *Clavessin auf welchem das piano forte zu haben*.

[2] Sachs, *Handbuch*, p. 149.

[3] Engel, *Mus. Times*, p. 469.

[4] Rees, article *Harpsichord*, written by Burney.

[5] Burney was employed for a time by Greville to teach him the harpsichord on the recommendation of old Kirkman, the harpsichord-maker, at whose house they met. Mme. D'Arblay, *Memoirs of Doctor Burney*, i, pp. 24 *ff.*, 1832.

[6] These were known in the trade as the " twelve apostles." Pohlmann, Buntebart, Beyer, Beck, Ganer, Schrader, Hartz, and others (see the Appendix) were probably amongst them. Many of their pianos still exist.

short time for Shudi,[1] but in 1761, at the latest, he started a business of his own and the making of square pianos in England began.[2] Their novelty, even in 1767, is recalled by the often-quoted play-bill, dated 16th May of that year, which states that at the end of the first act of the *Beggar's Opera* at Covent Garden, Miss Brickler will sing for her " benefit " a favourite song from *Judith* " accompanied by Mr. Dibdin [3] on a new instrument called Piano Forte." But they soon became extremely popular, and in ten years they were common. In Dublin, for instance, the piano was used by everyone according to Michael Kelly's description, in his *Reminiscences*, of the state of music in that city in 1777. These charming little instruments are only from three and a half to four and a half feet in length; the case, usually unornamented save for a line of inlay, rests unattached upon a trestle stand (Pl. LVII); the compass is usually five octaves less one note; and the wrest pins are on the extreme right of the soundboard in direct imitation of the clavichord. Zumpe's action is of remarkable simplicity. When the key is depressed, the hammer underneath the string is raised by a stout piece of wire with a leather stud at the end, known as " the old man's head," which is fixed into the key-lever. By the same action the hinged wooden damper, which rests on top of the string, is lifted by a thin piece of whalebone called the " mopstick ": this also is fixed into the key-lever. There are no pedals but the dampers, collectively divided into two sections, can be lifted off by the movement of two hand stops, of which the brass knobs are situated in a small box immediately on the left of the keyboard. A third stop was sometimes made to act as a mute: it brought a strip of leather into contact with the strings and was known as the sourdine.

This description of the square piano is applicable to most instruments made before about 1780, as they varied little and there was no great change in their construction except for a gradual increase in the size of the case and the abolition of the trestle-stand in favour of the " French frame " with its square tapering legs (Pl. LX). For some inexplicable reason they—and, in-

---

[1] Rees, *op. cit.*

[2] The date has always hitherto been given as between 1760 and 1765. An inspection of the rate-books of Princes St., Hanover Square, shows the regular entry of Zumpe's name from 1761 to 1780, when he moved to Princess St., Cavendish Square (see the Appendix). This admits Fetis's statement that he learned to play on one of Zumpe's pianos, dated 1762.

[3] This was Charles Dibdin, the composer of numerous operas and sea-songs, including *Lionel and Clarissa* and *Tom Bowling. Judith* was an oratorio written by Arne in 1764, at the performance of which, at Covent Garden in 1773, female voices were used for the first time in oratorio.

deed, any instrument prior to about 1800—are invariably called spinets by their owners, auctioneers, antique-dealers, and even musicians: they are also frequently converted into dressing-tables and sideboards, care being taken to remove the name-board and any other evidence of historic interest. In 1780 John Broadwood, the harpsichord-maker, who had made square pianos from 1773 onwards, entirely remodelled Zumpe's action and patented an improved and reconstructed instrument in 1783. He moved the wrest-plank to the back of the case opposite the keyboard, and brought the compass up to five octaves. Pedals were substituted in the patent for the hand-controlled levers which lifted the dampers, but they did not come into general use on the square piano until the nineteenth century. Crank-shaped under-dampers of brass replaced the old " mopstick " arrangement, but their inventor thought it fit to paste a label on the soundboard giving in French and English this pertinent advice: " If any of the dampers should rattle put a little oyl on the center. If any hammer should stick, press the pin that guides it on one side or the other till it plays free." The fact that this label was printed in both languages reminds us that the English square piano was held in high esteem in France where Anglomania was a fashionable disease at this time: [1] indeed the *pianos anglais*, as they were called, were so much in demand that it was not until 1777 that Erard made the first French square piano. Broadwood's alterations did not include the incorporation of the hopper into the action, but three years later (1786) John Geib, a craftsman working for the firm of Longman and Broderip,[2] remedied this omission. As the century progressed an ever increasing number of these instruments was made: [3] they were compact and easy to move, but it was evident that they

[1] The extracts made by de Bricqueville from the *Affiches, annonces et avis divers*, again throw light on the matter: *Beau forte-piano par un ouvrier qui arrive de Londres . . . Piano de Zump*, 22 *louis* [about £18, equivalent to about £80 to-day]. . . . *Très bon forte-piano à vendre ou troquer contre un violin de Stradivarius, d'Amati*, 25 *août*, 1782. It is evident that Zumpe enjoyed an international reputation, and the offer made in the last extract, to exchange a square piano for a Stradivari violin provides an interesting example of the relative value of musical instruments at this date.

[2] A firm of dealers in instruments and music-publishers whose output was enormous. Longman started his business about 1767 and took Lukey into partnership in 1771. Broderip joined them about 1777 and Lukey's name disappeared two years later. They became bankrupt in 1795. The pianist, Muzio Clementi, then joined Longman, who set up by himself again in 1802, and after a succession of partners (see Grove, article *Clementi*) the firm became Clementi & Co., and then Collard & Collard.

[3] An examination of Broadwood's books reveals (Dale, p. 10) that while the two Shudis and John Broadwood made just over 1100 harpsichords in sixty-four years, the same

would never be capable of a large full tone. Although instrument makers were bent on gradation rather than volume of tone, and never conceived the possibility of the luxurious notes of our modern instruments, they probably visualized a latent power in the grand piano.

The earliest pianos of this shape were, we have seen, very similar to the harpsichord in outline, and the English craftsmen also modelled a few experimental instruments on the harpsichord,[1] but unfortunately a specimen has not survived. Once again it was the ingenuity of a foreigner that established the manufacture in this country. The Dutchman, Americus Backers, had probably studied Silbermann's or some German version of Cristofori's action which he perfected with the help of John Broadwood, and his apprentice Robert Stodart, who took out a patent in the year 1777 in which the term " grand " was first used.[2] Backers' improvements, made about 1772, consisted of the removal of Cristofori's intermediary under-hammer—thus allowing the hopper to work directly on the notch in the butt of the hammer— and the introduction of a small button on the end of a screw, the adjustment of which changed the angle of the hopper thus controlling the distance of the escapement. This direct lever action was always known as the " English action," and it still forms the basis of the intricate mechanism which is demanded by modern piano technique. There were three strings to each note, and pedals were added some time after Broadwood's patent of 1783.[3]

firm produced 7000 square pianos and 1000 grand pianos between 1782 and 1802. Square pianos continued to be made until about 1860. They were built into commodes (Pl. LVIII) and made in the form of semicircular side-tables (Pl. LIX): a catalogue from Longman & Broderip, dated March 1790, advertises " Piano Fortes in Commodes, Side Boards and Dressing Tables for convenience of small rooms."

[1] After the arrival in London of Johann Christian Bach—Sebastian's youngest son—in 1762, harpsichord-makers were incited by his preference for the piano to make, not the new square pianos just introduced by Zumpe but a form of the grand piano. Burney, writing in Rees's *Cyclopaedia*, says: " After Bach's arrival all the harpsichord-makers in this country tried their mechanical powers on pianofortes, but the first attempts were always on the large size." Bach used these new pianos at the concerts he gave in conjunction with Abel, the celebrated *gamba* player.

[2] It was not generally used until about 1790: before then they were always called " large pianos."

[3] The soft pedal of this patent was of the continental type, known as the celeste, that damped the strings by interposing a strip of soft material, but some time during the next ten years the far more popular " shifting " soft pedal was introduced. The invention of this is usually attributed to the German maker Stein, but it was either copied or independently invented in England, for in 1787 one Humphry Walton patented a pedal for making the hammer strike one, two, or three strings. This was effected by moving the whole keyboard, and was made possible by the comparative narrowness of the hammer-heads which were

The usual harpsichord compass of five octaves, F—F, was retained until about 1791, when it was extended upwards to C: in 1794 bass notes were added down to C making six octaves,[1] but the graceful outlines of the case were still preserved (Pl. LXII).

The history of the grand piano has so far been its progress in England, and while the English instruments were certainly favoured by the ever-increasing number of pianists another type of action, which had appeared in both square and grand pianos about the same time as that of Backers, must not be overlooked. This was a South German action known as the *Prellmechanik*, which was subsequently improved in Vienna under the influence of the great school of Viennese composers and was called the German or Viennese action. It differed fundamentally from the English action, inas-

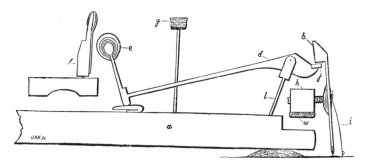

VIENNESE ACTION

much as the axis of the hammer was not fixed but rose with the key-lever (*a*), at the end of which was a short strip of wood (*l*) having a slot wherein the hammer-butt (*d*) was centred. In the earliest pianos with this type of action the blow was given to the hammer by the back of the butt hitting a projecting rail which was fixed at the back of the key.[2] The hammer head (*e*) therefore

covered with hard leather and not the thick felt to which we are accustomed to-day. The use of one string only was signified in the score by the term *una corda*, and the sympathetic vibration of the untouched strings produced a pleasant quality of tone. The loud pedal was divided so that only one half of the dampers could be lifted if desired— a device which lasted until about 1830.

[1] Shudi had made some of his harpsichords with the extension to C in the bass, but Kirkman, always more conservative, never departed from the usual five octaves. Broadwood made a piano of six octaves for Dussek in 1794, and Southwell of Dublin patented an upright piano of this compass in the same year.

[2] The diagram shows a later and more developed action, which belongs to a piano made by Nannette Streicher in 1823. Here there is a fixed hopper (*b*) regulated by an escapement button (*k*) and a hopper-spring (*i*).

pointed towards, instead of away from, the player; the check (*f*) being suitably situated. The damper (*g*) is of the "mopstick" type. While this action lacked the susceptibility to the player's mood, which was the most important feature of the direct lever actions already described, it certainly favoured a brilliant technique, and the touch was much lighter. The maker with whom its development was primarily associated was Johann Andreas Stein (1728-1792) [1] of Augsburg. His son Andreas took the invention to Vienna, and his daughter Nannette—a practical piano-maker, as well as a professional pianist—also moved there with her husband Johann Streicher.[2] Together they brought the Viennese action to its highest point of development in the early years of the nineteenth century. Weber, writing to his great friend the composer Gansbacher in 1813, says:

> I have bought two splendid instruments, one from Streicher and the other from Brodmann. In the course of the one day I saw at least fifty different ones of Schanz, Walter, Wachtl, etc., not one being worth a charge of powder compared with either of those I got.

Schanz and Walter were both imitators of Stein and were respectively the favourite makers of Haydn [3] and Mozart (Pl. LXI). The differences between the English and Viennese actions were shown up by the famous contest held in 1781 between Mozart and Clementi, but in spite of the inability of the audience to declare the winner, the English pianos were always regarded as the better. Beethoven preferred the grand given to him by the Broadwoods in 1817 to any other instrument. The other most important contributor to the history of the grand piano was Sebastien Erard who—we have already seen—made the first French square piano. He made his first grand piano in 1796,[4] and in 1808 he patented an action which contained the germ of the double escapement. This provided for a quick repetition of the stroke by releasing

---

[1] See Kinsky, p. 290, for a short biography. Pianos made by him are in the collections at Leipzig and Brussels, dated 1771 and 1780 respectively. He invented *genouillères* (knee-levers) in the place of foot-pedals, in addition to the shifting soft-pedal action already described.

[2] In 1808 he improved his instruments according to suggestions made by Beethoven.

[3] Haydn preferred Schanz's instruments because he found that although their tone was softer, the balance between treble and bass was better.

[4] Pascal Taskin, the famous harpsichord-maker, first made grand pianos in France. There is a grand made by him in 1787 (Sachs, Berlin Cat., Pl. x), and he also imported English pianos which were so popular in France at this time. Dale (p. 70) gives the following extract from Broadwood's books: "23 Oct. 1784. Pascall Taskian. 4 Pianos, one plain, 3 inlaid without stand, shipped to Paris."

the key only a very short distance—the normal action of modern instruments —but it was not perfected until 1821, when his nephew Pierre patented it. Another maker in France in the early nineteenth century was Ignaz Pleyel, a mediocre Austrian composer who moved to Paris and opened a factory in 1807. His reputation was partly due to his ingenious workman Henri Pape, who subsequently started a business of his own.

In addition to the square and grand piano we must consider a third form—the upright piano—which, by reason of the economy of space it effects, received special attention from instrument makers. The idea was not new, as we know from the existence of the mediaeval *clavicytherium* and the upright harpsichords of the eighteenth century, which have already been described, and when it was first applied to the piano the result was merely a vertical grand piano. Instruments of this kind were made in Germany in the middle of the eighteenth century,[1] but were never very popular there or in Austria. In the last decade of the century they were constructed to resemble a book-case,[2] and were called cabinet pianos, but it was not till 1800 that the idea of extending the strings below the level of the keyboard to the floor received practical fulfilment. In that year John Isaac Hawkins patented his upright piano,[3] both in this country and in the United States where he was living at the time, and where piano-making was soon to develop entirely on its own lines.[4] He was fortunate in attracting the attention of Thomas Jefferson, third President of the United States, whose love of music is commented upon by his biographers. In a letter to his daughter written at Philadelphia [5] in 1800 Jefferson says:

A very ingenious, modest and poor young man in Philadelphia, has

[1] There is an upright grand piano at Brussels made by Friederici in 1745. Other types of the upright piano made in Germany and Austria were the Pyramidenflügel and, in the early years of the nineteenth century, the Giraffenflügel. The latter name was also given to the upright pianos, known in England as cabinet pianos (Pl. LXV), which were popular between about 1810 and 1825.

[2] Southwell of Dublin, a most ingenious craftsman with many patents to his credit, invented an upright square piano (figured in *Dict. Eng. Furniture*, iii, 6), and William Stodart's popular bookcase piano (Pl. LXIII) was patented in 1795.

[3] These instruments are about five and a half feet high, and the frame containing the keyboard is pivoted in the manner of the falling front of a bureau to economize space.

[4] Inasmuch as the history of keyboard instruments in America virtually begins with the piano it only remains to notice the consistent importation of European instruments and the occasional emigration of European craftsmen. In the eighteenth century a few spinets and harpsichords were made (Pl. XXXII).

[5] E. Singleton, *The furniture of our forefathers*, 1901.

invented one of the prettiest improvements in the pianoforte that I have seen, and it has tempted me to engage one for *Monticello*. His strings are perpendicular, and he contrives within that height to give his strings the same length as in a grand pianoforte, and fixes the three unisons to the same screw. It scarcely gets out of tune at all, and then, for the most part, the three unisons are tuned at once.

The next step in the advancement of this invention was the increase of the length of the strings by placing them diagonally instead of vertically— an idea patented by Thomas Loud in 1802. In 1811 a lower model about four feet in height, known subsequently as the "Cottage Piano," was invented by Robert Wornum—a type in which ugliness found its apotheosis in the Victorian age. It was introduced to France in 1815 by Pleyel.

Hawkins had included in his piano another innovation of paramount importance. This was the substitution of iron for the customary wooden frame, but it was not until 1820 that there was a real recognition of the tremendous increase of tension, and the consequent use of thicker and heavier strings, made possible by this change. In this year William Allen and James Thom, a tuner and foreman employed by William Stodart, patented a metal frame for the grand piano [1] which met with general approbation, and at this point the instrument enters upon a new phase of technical improvement which is beyond the scope of this work.

The rapidity of the development of the piano in the thirty years before 1820 is truly astonishing when we compare with it the leisurely progress through the centuries of the harpsichord and clavichord. But instrumental performance was now on the increase and had become a pretty accomplishment, together with japanning and shell-work. A contemporary dictionary of etiquette [2]—in which correct deportment at the pianoforte would, of course, be included—sums up the matter in these words:

Le nombre de personnes qui excellent sur cet instrument est hors de proportion avec les virtuoses de tous les autres: c'est que la commodité de son attitude permet, sans nulle fatigue, des études de sept ou huit heures. Les grands talens sur le clavecin étoient jadis plus rares, qu'ils ne le sont aujourd'hui sur le piano; d'abord parce que le goût de la musique etait

[1] Stodart immediately bought the patent but refused to enforce its observance lest further improvements in construction by other craftsmen should be hindered (Hipkins, p. 16).
[2] *Dictionnaire des étiquettes*, by Madame de Genlis, 1813.

moins général, ensuite parce que le clavecin n'avait véritablement qu'un genre, la vitesse; enfin, parce que sa grandeur le rendoit fort incommode dans un petit appartement.

This was the period of Romanticism, and the piano is essentially a romantic instrument, its dynamic gradation of tone catching the popular and romantic imagination at a moment when change in everything was inevitable. The natural reaction from the intense artificiality of the eighteenth century brought with it a period of unrest when a desire for truth led, amongst other things, to a return to mediaevalism, of which the Gothic Revival was the natural out-come.[1] The satires of Pope and Gay were laid aside for the lyrics of Keats and Shelley, the elegant make-believe of Watteau and Fragonard for the impassioned realism of Géricault and Delacroix, the academic restraint of Bach and Handel for the emotional spontaneity of Weber and Schubert. Form in music no longer assumed an undue importance at the expense of matter, and matter sought to clothe itself in a new form, until the two were united in an indissoluble partnership in the person of the greatest musician the world has ever known—Ludwig van Beethoven. In the dual capacity of composer and performer he was the first real exponent of the piano; and his name must be associated with the instrument as definitely as that of Chopin.

To remark the undoubted revival of interest in these early instruments makes a fitting conclusion to this work. Not only is their history receiving attention to-day, but curiosity has so far quickened as to encourage a few craftsmen to return to the plucked string and the tangent, and to rediscover the beauties of *grand jeu* [2] and *Bebung*. While it is not suggested that the future development of music will demand their more frequent use, it is at least possible with their aid to have a better understanding of that vast mass of first-rate music from Byrd to Mozart, which loses much of its character by being played on a piano, and to gratify a very proper desire to recapture the sounds of a performance of it during the life-time of the composer. The instruments being made to-day, although they cannot have the mellowness and dignity which Time alone bestows, can benefit by the application of modern scientific knowledge; and if the craftsmen of to-day can, without

[1] The influence of this movement on the applied arts is an interesting and sometimes distressing study (Pl. LXIV).

[2] The harpsichordist's term to denote the use of all the resources of the instrument, *cf.* " full organ."

too flagrant a violation of antiquarian principles, make them more reliable and less sensitive to climatic conditions they will receive the gratitude of those who hold the belief—which has directed my choice of a frontispiece— that the perfect interpretation of an eighteenth-century saraband can be obtained by the use of a twentieth-century harpsichord.

APPENDIX

APPENDIX

THE dates in this List—which does not claim to be complete—are taken from existing instruments, directories, newspaper cuttings, parish registers, rate-books, patents, etc.: the actual date of birth or death when known is signified by the letters *b.* and *d.* The abbreviation *fl.* (floruit) signifies that only one date is known. The instruments known to have been made by each maker are abbreviated as follows: virginal *V*, spinet *S*, harpsichord *H*, clavichord *C*, pianos square and grand *P*, square pianos *Ps*, grand pianos *Pg*, claviorganum *Cl*, i.e. a combination of a small organ and a spinet, harpsichord, or even piano. The use of a particular letter does not denote that the maker only made that kind of instrument, or that he only made keyboard instruments. When an address is given the town is always London unless otherwise stated.

Maker	Address	Earliest and latest dates known	Remarks
ADAM, Alexander (V)		*fl.* 1659	See Grove, article *Virginal.*
ADLAM, John. (P)	40 King's St., Soho	*fl.* 1793	
ASTON, ——. (H)	Prince's Arms, New Queen St.	*fl.* 1730	
ASTOR, George. (Ps)	79 Cornhill	*c.* 1785–1810	Early in the 19th century the firm became Astor & Horwood.
BACKERS, Americus. (Pg)	Jermyn St.	*c.* 1767–*c.* 1781	See p. 54.

63

Maker	Address	Earliest and latest dates known	Remarks
BALL, James. (P)	Duke St., Grosvenor Sq.	1790–1817	
BARTON, Thomas. (S, H)	The Crown, Bishopsgate St.	1714–1731	See footnote below, and p. 38.
BAUDIN, Joseph. (S)		*fl.* 1723	A spinet of this date is figured in Rimbault, p. 69.
BECK, Frederick. (Ps)	4 Broad St., Golden Square 10 Broad St., Golden Square	1774–1794	A piano dated 1789 bears the number 2000! See Pl. LVIII.
BELL, ——. (P)	Charles Square, Hoxton	*fl.* 1800	
BEYER, Adam. (Cl, Ps)	Compton St., Soho Square	1774–1795	He also made piano-organs, *e.g.* Bruni, Nos. 32 and 150.
BLAIR, WOOD & Co. (Ps)	Edinburgh		
BLANCKART, Jasper. (V)	Aldgate	1566-1582	See p. 29.
BLAND & WELLER. (P)	23 Oxford Street	1802-1817	
BLUMER, Samuel. (S, H)	Great Pulteney St., Golden Sq.	1749-1788	At one time foreman to Shudi. See Pl. XLIX, and Dale, p. 50.

In the issue of *The Craftsman* for 6th March 1730/1 the following notice is printed: "Whereas it is confidently reported, That THOMAS BARTON, Harpsichord Maker, has left off his Trade and keeps a Tavern: This is to assure the Publick the said Report is utterly false and groundless; and that he still continues his Business (which he never had Thought of declining) at the Crown near the South Sea House, Bishopsgate-Street, to make all Sorts of Harpsichords and Spinets, particularly his late invented upright Harpsichord, and to perform all things appertaining to that Business."

Maker	Address	Earliest and latest dates known	Remarks
BLUNT, Edward. (S)		1664–1703	See *infra*, note 1.
BRACKLEY, Charles. (S)		*c.* 1700	One of his spinets is figured in *Dict. of English Furniture*, iii, 3.
BROADWOOD, John. (H, P)	32 Great Pulteney St., Golden Sq.	*b.* 1732–*d.* 1812	See pp. 42, 53-4.
BRODERIP & WILKINSON. (Ps)	13 Haymarket	1798–1811	See Grove, article *Broderip & Wilkinson*.
BUCKINGER, Joseph. (P)	443 Strand	1793–1809	
BUNTEBART, Gabriel. (Ps)	7 Princes St., Hanover Sq.	1769–1795	See *infra*, note 2, and Pl. LVII.
BURY, SAMUEL, & Co. (P)	113 Bishopsgate-within	1787–1794	
BUTCHER, Thomas. (P)	41 Gt. Titchfield St.	*c.* 1810–1821	
BUTT, John. (P)	Finsbury Market		
CALDER, Alexander	Aberdeen	*c.* 1820	
CELSON, Ephraim (H)			Only known from an announcement [3] in the *Public Ledger*, 2nd Oct. 1778.

[1] On the first key of one of his spinets is written: "Thos. Hitchcock his make in 1664"; and on the first jack of another, formerly in the Taphouse collection, is inscribed: "Thos. Hitchcock No. 54—1703." It seems, therefore, that the Hitchcocks made instruments for Blunt, who was perhaps only a dealer, but see p. 31, note 1.

[2] From 1780-1795 he appears in the rate-books at Zumpe's old address. From about 1790 he was joined by Sievers, and one of their pianos is at the Musée Instrumental, Brussels.

[3] "To be sold by Christie & Ansell . . . (Earl Ferrers dec^d. effects). . . . A remarkable fine toned Harpsichord by EPHRAIM CELSON, an instrument of a most extraordinary Construction and justly esteemed the most compleat Harpsichord in the Kingdom: it con-

Maker	Address	Earliest and latest dates known	Remarks
CHEW, ——. (H)	Bristol (?)	*fl.* 1780	
CHILD, Francis. (H)		*fl.* 1749	In a Westminster poll book.
CLEMENTI & Co. (P)	26 Cheapside 195 Tottenham Court Rd.	1798–1832	See Grove, article *Clementi & Co.*
CORRIE, ——. (P)	41 Broad St., Golden Square	*fl.* 1794	
COSTON, Francis. (H)	Brownlow St., Drury Lane	*c.* 1700–1738	A harpsichord of the early 18th century, formerly in the Boddington collection, was attributed to him. He sold his stock-in-trade in 1738.
CRANG, ——. (Cl)	London	*fl.* 1745	The combination of organ and harpsichord was revived in the eighteenth century.
CULLIFORD, Thomas. (S, H, Ps)	112 Cheapside 172 Strand	1750–*c.* 1800	He worked[1] for Longman & Broderip (*q.v.*), and also with Rolfe & Barrow (*q.v.*) as Culliford & Co.
DALE, Joseph. (Ps)	19 Cornhill 132 Oxford St.	1792–1808	One of his pianos has Ganer's name stamped on the case. Probably a dealer.

tains a double Bass, two Unisons and an Octave, the Welch Harp, Piano Forte and Celestial Harp: and a matchless Cabinet inlaid with Tortoise-shell and ornamented with Or Boulu [*sic*].'' In the list of stops the '' double Bass '' may be a 16 ft. tone stop, and the '' Welch Harp '' is the ordinary buff or harp stop.

[1] A harpsichord in the Henry Watson collection, Manchester, bears Longman's and Broderip's names on the nameboard, but when the soundboard was repaired the following inscription in pencil was found on its back: *Thomas Culliford, Maker, April,* 1780. *No.* 12.''

Maker	Address	Earliest and latest dates known	Remarks
DAVIDSON, John. (V)		*fl.* 1652	See Grove, article *Virginal*.
DAVIS, John. (Pg)	11 Catherine St., Strand	*fl.* 1817	
DETTMER, GEORGE, & SON. (Ps)	50 Upper Marylebone St.	*c.* 1805–1817	
DIERKES, Charles. (Ps)	7 Percy St., Bedford Square	*c.* 1810–1825	
DONE, Joshua. (Ps)	30 Chancery Lane	1793–1794	
DONNER, John. (H)		*fl.* 1793	In list of subscribers to Sheraton's *Cabinet-Maker*.
DOWNING, George. (H)	234 Strand	1763–1783	
EDWARDS,——. (Ps)	Lambeth		
ELWICK,——. (H)	Long Acre	*fl.* 1794	
ERARD, Sébastien. (P)	18 Great Marlborough St.	*b.* 1752–*d.* 1831	Worked in London intermittently from 1786 to 1815, when he left his English shop in the charge of his nephew Pierre.
EVENDEN & SONS. (Ps)		*c.* 1820	
FAIRN, Alex. (H)		*fl.* 1793	Subscriber to Sheraton's *Cabinet-Maker*.
FAULKNER,——. (H)	Salisbury Court, Fleet St.	1760–1769	See footnote below, and p. 43, n. 2.

Dow (p. 298) quotes the *Boston Gazette*, 27th June 1763: " Lewis Deblois of Boston advertised for sale a curious Ton'd, double key'd, new harpsichord, just imported in Capt. *Millard* from London. Is esteem'd the Master Piece of the famous Falconer [*sic*].''

Maker	Address	Earliest and latest dates known	Remarks
FENTON, ——. (S)		*c.* 1700	Quoted by Rimbault (p. 60) as spinet-maker.
FROESCHLE, George. (P)	21 Mark Lane	1788–1800	Worked with Satchell.
GANER, Christopher (S, Ps)	22 Broad St., Golden Square 48 and 49 Broad St., Golden Sq.	1774–1809	
GARBUTT, J. (P)	8 Bolsover St., Oxford St.	*fl.* 1793	Probably son of T. Garbutt.
GARBUTT, T. (H, P)	King St., Golden Square	*fl.* 1775	
GARCKA, George. (Ps)	Stephen St., Rathbone Place	1788–1793	
GEIB, John. (H, P)	Old Bailey	*c.* 1775–1807	See note below, and p. 53.
GERBER, William. (H)		*fl.* 1775	A harpsichord of this date is numbered 115.
GIBSON, William. (H)	Dublin	1764–1776	See WOFFINGTON.
GILCHRIST, Doug'ld. (H)		*fl.* 1793	Subscriber to Sheraton's *Cabinet Maker.*
GILLESPY, Samuel. (H)	Brownlow St., St. Giles-in-the-Fields.	1769–1774	Patent No. 1092.
GLANVILLE, George. (H)		*fl.* 1749	In a Westminster poll book.

Some of his early instruments bear the signature GEIB & GOLDSWORTH, and he was in business with Lenkfeld (*q.v.*) for a time. He also patented a combined piano and clavichord (Patent No. 1866). By 1798 he had emigrated to New York (see *Antiques*, xvi, p. 112).

Maker	Address	Earliest and latest dates known	Remarks
GOULDING, D'ALMAINE & POTTER. (Ps)	20 Soho Square and Westmore-land St., Dublin.	c. 1785–1801	By 1801 firm known as Goulding, Phipps & D'Almaine, and worked at 117 New Bond St.
GRAY, Robert & William. (H)	72 Queen Ann St. East	*fl.* 1793	Their trade card is figured in Pl. XLIX.
HANCOCK, John Crang. (P)	32 Parliament St., Westminster 82 Wych St., St. Clement Danes	1779–1794	Patent No. 1743. He also made a few pianos in the shape of spinets. Messrs. Broadwood have one.
HANCOCK, Thomas. (S)	London	c. 1700	
HARDY, Henry. (P)	Oxford	c. 1800	
HARRIS, Baker. (S, H, Ps)	London	1760–1780	Specialized in spinets.
HARRIS, John. (S, H)	Red Lion St., Holborn and Boston, Mass.	1730–1769	He went to Boston in 1768.
HARRIS, Joseph. (S, H)	London	1750–c. 1765	Father of John Harris. See Pl. XXXI.
HARRIS, William. (S, H)	44 Fetter Lane	1773–1793	
HARRISON, John. (S)		1749–1757	
HARROD, R.	Fore St., Exeter	*fl.* 1795	
HATLEY, Robert. (V)		c. 1650	See Grove, article *Virginal.*

Maker	Address	Earliest and latest dates known	Remarks
HAWARD, Charles. (S, H)	Aldgate St.	*c.* 1660–1687	The name is variously spelled HAYWARD or HAWARD. See p. 30.
HAWARD, John. (V, H)		1622–1676	See p. 120.
HAWARD, Thomas. (V)	Bishopsgate	*fl.* 1656	
HAXBY, Thomas. (S, H, Ps)	Blake St., York	*c.* 1737–*c.* 1798	For a detailed account of him, see *Mus. Antiq.*, ii, 56.
HEROCK, T.	Gracechurch St.	*c.* 1810	
HICKS, Peter. (C)		*c.* 1720	See Pl. XIV.
HILBERG, ——. (H)			A harpsichord offered for sale in *The World*, 27 March 1788.
HITCHCOCK, John. (S, H)		1743–*d.* 1774	See pp. 31, 124.
HITCHCOCK, Thomas. (S, H)		1690–1715	See Pl. XLIV, and p. 31.
HOLLAND, Henry. (Ps)	Bedford Row	1783–1798	A fine piano illustrated in Jourdain's *English Decoration and Furniture of the later XVIIIth century.*
HOLLISTER, Thomas. (H)	Dublin	*fl.* 1728	
HOLLISTER, William Castell. (H)	40 Cuffe St., Dublin	1766–1781	
HOLMES, James. (P)	Bridge St., Norwich	*fl.* 1795	

Maker	Address	Earliest and latest dates known	Remarks
HOPTON, Heming. (H)	Rupert St.	*fl.* 1749	In a Westminster poll book.
HOUSTON & Co. (S, H, P)	54 Great Marlborough St.	1790-1794	
JAMES, John. (V)		*fl.* 1571	
JONES, Philip. (V, H)		*fl.* 1671	See Grove, article *Virginal*, and note below.
JONES, ROUND & Co. (P)	11 Golden Sq.	1804–1808	Formerly R. Jones. See Pl. XLIV.
KEENE, Stephen. (V, S, H)	Threadneedle St.	1668–1719	See p. 30, and Grove, article *Virginal*.
KEMYS, John. (H)	Small St., then King St., Bristol	*fl.* 1752	
KIRKMAN, Jacob, Abraham, Joseph. (H, S, P)	Great Pulteney St. 19 Broad St., Golden Square	1739–1896	Only one spinet known. See Pl. I., p. 43, and Grove, article *Kirkman*.
KIRSHAW, John. (S)	Manchester	*c.* 1740	A spinet at Goodrich Court.
KNOWLES & ALLEN. (Ps)	Aberdeen		
LANDRETH, John. (P)		*fl.* 1787	
LAWSON, HENRY, & Co. (P)	29 John St., Fitzroy Square		

In the sale catalogue of the music and instruments of Thomas Britton, the musical small-coal man, which were sold after his death in 1714, is " a good harpsichord by Philip Jones."

Maker	Address	Earliest and latest dates known	Remarks
LE BLOND, William. (Ps)	London and Dunkirk	*c.* 1780–1792	A piano dated 1789 is inscribed *Nunc Dunkercae.*
LEE, John and Edward. (H)	Dublin	1790–*c.* 1800	
LENKFELD, Ludwig. (Ps)	Tottenham Court Rd.	*c.* 1790–1796	In business with GEIB for some years until 1796 when partnership was dissolved.
LEVERSIDGE, Adam. (V)	London	1666–1670	See Grove, article *Virginal.*
LINCOLN, John. (H)	199 High Holborn	*fl.* 1793	
LOGIER, John Bernard.	27 Lower Sackville St., and 46 Upper Sackville St., etc., Dublin	*b.* 1780–*d.* 1846	Inventor of the chiroplast,[1] patent No. 3806. See Grove.
LONGMAN, James, & BRODERIP, Francis Fane. (S, H, P)	26 Cheapside 13 Haymarket 195 Tottenham Court Rd.	1767–1795	See p. 53, Pl. LX, also Grove. They became bankrupt in 1795.
LONGMAN & LUKEY. (S)	26 Cheapside	1771–1777	See p. 53, note 2.
LOOSEMOORE, John. (V)	Exeter	*b.* 1613–*d.* 1681	Also a famous organ-builder. See Grove, article *Virginal.*
LOUD, Thomas. (P)	22 Devonshire St., Queen's Sq.	1802–1825	Patent No. 2591. The violinist Felix Yaniewicz was in the business for a period. In 1825 Loud settled in Philadelphia.
LUXTON, Richard. (V)	" of St. Ethelborrowe's "	*fl.* 1611	

[1] An apparatus which could be fitted to a pianoforte to ensure correct position of the hand and movement of the fingers. There is one at Stranger's Hall, Norwich, which has been figured and described by F. Leney in *The Connoisseur,* lxvi, 94.

Maker	Address	Earliest and latest dates known	Remarks
MacDonnell, Alexander, James, & Daniel. (H)	12 Anglesea St., Dublin	1790–1804	
Maddey, ——. (H)	Custom House Lane, Queen Square, Bristol	*c.* 1785	
Mahoon, Joseph.	York Buildings and " King's Arms, North side of Golden Square."	1735–1771 [1]	In Hogarth's *Rake's Progress* (2nd plate painted in 1735) there is a harpsichord by him.
Merlin, John Joseph. (H, Ps)	69 Queen Ann St., East. Princes St., Hanover Square	*b.* 1735–*d.* 1804	Arrived in England in 1760 and lived at first address until 1779. Patent No. 1081. See Rimbault, pp. 92-3.
Monro & May. (P)	60 Skinner St., Snow Hill, Holborn Bars	1793–1827	Probably John Monro and Charles May, both of whom were piano-makers: the latter left Longman & Broderip in 1788 and set up on his own.
Moore, William. (P)		*c.* 1785	
Moore, ——. (Ps)	45 Ranelagh St., Liverpool		
Morland, ——. (H)	Dublin		
Mott, Isaac, Henry, Robert. (P)	73 Pall Mall	1817–1825	Invented a " Sostinente Piano Forte," patent No. 4098.

[1] A spinet in the Victoria and Albert Museum has the inscription " 1771—No. 45 " written on the first key-lever. This is perhaps a workman's number, as the number of spinets he had made by this date must have exceeded forty-five.

Maker	Address	Earliest and latest dates known	Remarks
NAUBAUER, Frederick. (H)		*fl.* 1772	His stock-in-trade sold in this year. Rimbault, p. 88.
NEWBANE, ——. (H)	" Greek St., the corner of Compton St., Soho "	*fl.* 1773	Mentioned in an advertisement of the *Morning Post*, 26th July 1773.
PETHER, George. (H, P)	61 Oxford St., 16 John St., Oxford St.	*c.* 1775–1794	" From Mr. Kirkman's," inscribed on a square piano.
PLAYER, John. (S, H)		*c.* 1680–*c.* 1720	See Pl. XXIX.
PLENIUS, John. (S, H)	89 Holborn	1765–1793	
PLENIUS, Roger. (H)	South Audley St.	1741–1756	See pp. 40 and 51. He became bankrupt in 1756.
POHLMAN, Johann. (P)	Compton St., Soho 113 Gt. Russell St.	1767–1793	
PRESTON, John. (Ps)	97 Strand	1777–1794	Probably only a dealer.
PRINGLE, ——. (Pg)		*fl.* 1792	
REDPATH & DAVIDSON. (P)		*fl.* 1789	
RELFE, John. (S)		*c.* 1740	
REWALLIN, Charles. (V)	St. Sidwell's, Exeter	1657–*d.* 1697	See *Connoisseur*, xlvi, 77.
RICE, John. (H)	Dublin	*fl.* 1790	

Maker	Address	Earliest and latest dates known	Remarks
ROCHEAD, ANDREW, & SON. (Ps)	Greenside Place, Leith Walk, Edinburgh	1793–1821	
ROLFE, WILLIAM & SONS. (P)	112 Cheapside	1785–1839	In partnership until 1797 with Culliford (*q.v.*) and Barrow.
ROTHER, Henry. (H)	9 Gt. Booter Lane, Dublin	1774–1782	
RYLEY, Edward. (P)	Kingston-upon-Hull	*fl.* 1801	Queen Charlotte had a square piano.
SCHOENE & Co. (Ps)	Princes St., Cavendish Sq.	1784–1793	Took over Zumpe's business when he retired.
SCHRADER & HARTZ. (Ps)		*c.* 1768–1780	
SCOTT, Robert, John, and Alexander. (P)	29 Mortimer St., Cavendish Sq.	1801–1817	Patent No. 2552.
SCOULER, James, senr. (S, H)	Gt. Newport St.	1762–1788	James Scouler, junr., was a miniature painter.
SEEDE, Brice. (H)	Lewin's Mead, Bristol	1753–1772	
SELLS, ——. (H)		*c.* 1750	
SHUDI, Burkat. (H)	Meard St., Soho, and 32 Gt. Pulteney St., Golden Square	*b.* 1702–*d.* 1773	See pp. 40 *ff.*, and Pl. LII.
SHUDI, Burkat, junr. (H)		1740–*d.* 1803	See p. 42.

Maker	Address	Earliest and latest dates known	Remarks
SHUDI, Joshua. (H)	Silver St., Golden Square	*d.* 1774	See footnote below and Dale, p. 52. Silver St. is now known as Beak St.
SISON, Benjamin. (S, H)	Birchin Lane	*c.* 1700	A harpsichord in the Lady Lever Art Gallery, Port Sunlight.
SKEENE, ——. (H)		*fl.* 1779	
SLADE, Benjamin. (S, H)		*fl.* 1700	See Pl. XXX.
SMITH, John. (S, H)	20 Bridge St., Bristol	*fl.* 1775	
SMITH, John. (S)	College Wynd, Edinburgh	*c.* 1760	
SMITH, Joseph. (H)		*fl.* 1799	
SKEENE, ——. (H)			
SOUTHWELL, William (P)	26 Fleet St. 20 Marlborough St.	*b.* 1756–*d.* 1842	First apprenticed to Weber (*q.v.*). Numerous patents. See Flood, p. 139.
STEWART, Neil. (S, Ps)	Blackfriars Wynd, Edinburgh	1761–1791	A spinet at Goodrich Court.
STODART, Robert, William, Malcolm. (P)	Wardour St., Soho Golden Square	1776–1861	See Pl. LXIII, and Grove.

Nephew of Burkat Shudi. The only known instrument bearing his signature is dated .1776: this means that his widow Mary carried on the business still using his name. She moved to 16 Berwick St., Soho, and on 18th February 1780 retired to the country after selling her stock-in-trade " consisting of several capital double and single keyed Harpsichords & some unfinished: likewise a quantity of Mahogany & Walnut Tree Veneers, Work-Bench, Tools, & sundry other effects," as we learn from *The General Advertiser*, 5th February 1780.

Maker	Address	Earliest and latest dates known	Remarks
STRONG, Adrian. (V)	Dublin	1639–1655	Flood, p. 138.
TABEL, Herman. (H)	Swallow St., St. James's	1721–d. 1738	See p. 41. In contemporary press notices his name is often spelled TABLE.
TESTA, Andrea. (H)		1658–1668	"Harpsicall maker" to Charles II. (De Lafontaine, 208 and 465.) [1]
THEEWES, Ludovic.	St. Martin's Le Grand	1568–1579	See Pl. XXXVI.
THOMPSON, Charles, Samuel, Ann, Peter, etc. (S, H)	75 St. Paul's Churchyard, and 8 Lombard St.	1764–1802	
TISSERAND, Joseph. (H)	London	*c.* 1710	
TOMKISON, Thomas. (P)	55 Dean St., Soho	1800–1839	
TOWNSEND, Gabriel. (V)		*fl.* 1641	The only virginal known by him figured in *Dict. Eng. Furniture*, iii, 3.
TREASURER, William. (V)	"Christ Church Parish"	1521–1576	See p. 29.

[1] " In the Calendar of State Papers (Domestic Series) we have under date of 1668 a petition of Andrea to the King for a pension . . . 'as formerly granted to Gerolamo Zenti, harpsicall maker' whose place he supplies, being sent over by Zenti, who went to Paris, and died in the French King's service." There are two harpsichords by Zenti in the Crosby Brown collection (*Catalogue of keyboard instruments*, pp. 62 and 66), made at Rome and dated 1658 and 1666.

Maker	Address	Earliest and latest dates known	Remarks
TRUTE, Charles. (P)	7 Broad St., Golden Square	*fl.* 1793	
UNDERWOOD, Thomas. (S, H)	Market Place, Bath	1746–1760	
WALKER, Adam, D., and J. (H)	8 Great Pulteney St., Golden Square	1772–1781	Invented the Celestina, described in Patent No. 1020.[1]
WALTON, Humphry. (P)		*fl.* 1787	See p. 54, n. 3.
WARN, Thomas. (S, H)	Gloucester	*fl.* 1740	
WARRELL & Co. (Ps)	" Near Astley's Theatre, Westminster Bridge "	*c.* 1795	Also made organised pianos.[2]
WEBER, Ferdinand. (H, Ps)	Werburgh St., Dublin	1739–*d.* 1784	See Flood, pp. 139 *ff.*
WESTON, Thomas. (P)	John St., Golden Square	*fl.* 1793	
WHITE, James. (V)	Old Jewry	1656–1670	See Grove, article *Virginal*, and note 3 below.

[1] An advertisement for their " Celestina harpsichords " claims that " this pathetic stop expresses soft or sentimental music in tones sweeter than the musical glasses or the Eolian harp." A sostinente effect was aimed at by the use of a bow worked by hand.

[2] Their trade card in Mr. Heal's collection is inscribed as follows: " Square Piano Fortes superior to most others, however dignified and puffed off:—Grand Piano Fortes considerably under the usual enormous Prices:—Organised Piano Fortes on the same Philosophical Principles:—Organs, Harpsichords, Spinets and other Instruments Second-hand, on reasonable Terms."

[3] He was rewarded in 1670 by the Committee of the Royal Exchange for eminent services rendered in " stopping the fyre " [*i.e.* the Great Fire] at the Bartholomew Lane end of the building.

Maker	Address	Earliest and latest dates known	Remarks
WHITE, Thomas. (V)	Old Jewry	1651–d. 1660	See Grove, article *Virginal*.
WHITE, ——. (P)	1 Milsom St., 3 George St. Bath.	*fl.* 1800	
WILKINSON & WORNUM. (P)	315 Oxford St. 11 Prince's St., Hanover Square	1810–1812	Wornum was only in partnership for two years with Wilkinson, who was probably the same maker that joined with Broderip (*q.v.*).
WOFFINGTON, John, Robert. (H, P)	9 William St., Dublin	1728–1836	W. Gibson was in partnership with this firm.
WOOLFINDEN, John. (S)		*c.* 1725	
WORNUM, Robert, Jun. (P)		*b.* 1780–*d.*1852	In partnership with George Wilkinson (*q.v.*) 1810-12. See p. 58.
WRENSHALL, Joseph. (P)	49 Paradise St., Liverpool	1793-1795	
WRIGHT, W. (P)	High Bridge, Newcastle		
YANIEWICZ, Felix.			See LOUD.
ZOPFI, Hans Belthazar. (H)	King St., Golden Square	*d.* 1750	See p. 41, and note below.

A fellow-countryman of Shudi, whose niece he married (Dale, pp. 31 and 52). Beyond the fact that he died in 1750, Dale says there is nothing known of him, but in the *London Gazette*, 23rd February 1750, there is a notice to " all persons indebted to the estate of Mr. John Belthazar Zopffee [*sic*] . . . harpsichord-maker deceased." His trade is determined by this.

Maker	Address	Earliest and latest dates known	Remarks
Zumpe, Johann. (Ps)	7 Princess St., Hanover Square Princes St., Cavendish Sq.	1761–1780 1780–1784	See p. 51, and Pl. LVII.

The following notice is in the *General Advertiser*, 1st February 1780: " Mr. Zumpe, the inventor of the Small Piano-Forte and Maker to her Majesty and the Royal Family (removed from Princess Street, Hanover Square to Princes-Street, Cavendish Square) begs leave to acquaint the Nobility & Gentry, that he has just compleated a New Improvement, with different Pedals, that makes the Piano-Forte perfect in every degree, which hitherto it never was; and also prevents that instrument from going out of order, which was always the case before."

PLATES

PLATE I

PAGE FROM THE DĪVĀN OF ANVARI

Persian, 1515.

THIS scene represents an important person enjoying a musical party in a garden—a subject often chosen by Persian miniature painters of this period. One musician plays the harp and the other plays a psaltery (see p. 5, note 4). Although keyboard instruments were not made by the Persians they were imported from western countries, as we learn from the observations of European travellers. John Tavernier, for instance, a nobleman of France, tells us in his *Six Voyages . . . through Turky into Persia . . . finished in the year 1670,* that the King's instrumental music " consisted of a kind of a Lute, a Guittar, a Spinet, and two or three Base Flutes. He had also in the Gallery where the Curtisans were, a large Ebony Cabinet . . . which proved to be an Organ that went alone." In 1598 Queen Elizabeth sent an organ as a present to the Sultan of Turkey, which was conveyed under the personal supervision of Master Thomas Dallam, founder of the famous family of organ-builders of that name. (See " Master Dallam's Mission " in *The Antiquary,* vol. xviii.)

8 in. by 4 in.

Victoria and Albert Museum, London.

دوستی کنج سکون کن بر آ | صبر که روزود و خوب کند

آب رفته بجوی باز آید | کار بسته از انجه بود کند

گفتم آب رجویمی آیم | هی مراده ریه سود کند

هر طرف مشقت متندی می کشد لب

مرکب من که ردبشه بود | جان غذا کرد و حرکت پیش کرد

بینه

PLATE II

CARVED WOODEN FIGURE

English, c. 1370.

A SEATED figure of an angel playing a rectangular psaltery (see p. 6). This is one of the panels below the lowest row of stalls in the choir of Lincoln Cathedral, which contain alternately the figures of a king and an angel with a musical instrument. An approximate date can be given to these very fine stalls as they were erected at the order of John of Welbourn, Treasurer of the Cathedral between about 1350 and 1380, when he died.

Photo by S. Smith, Lincoln.

Lincoln Cathedral.

PLATE III

PAGE FROM THE LOUTERELL PSALTER

English, c. 1340.

IN this page (Psalm lxxix, verse 18 to Psalm lxxx, verse 4) of this famous manuscript the large initial E contains a miniature of King David playing the psaltery. The instrument is of the type known from its shape as *strumento di porco*, and he plays it with his fingers instead of with the little plectra often used.

There are several other representations of musical instruments in this manuscript which, although it shows the East Anglian school in its decadence, is particularly rich in illustrations of contemporary country life.

14 in. by 9⅞ in.

British Museum, London.

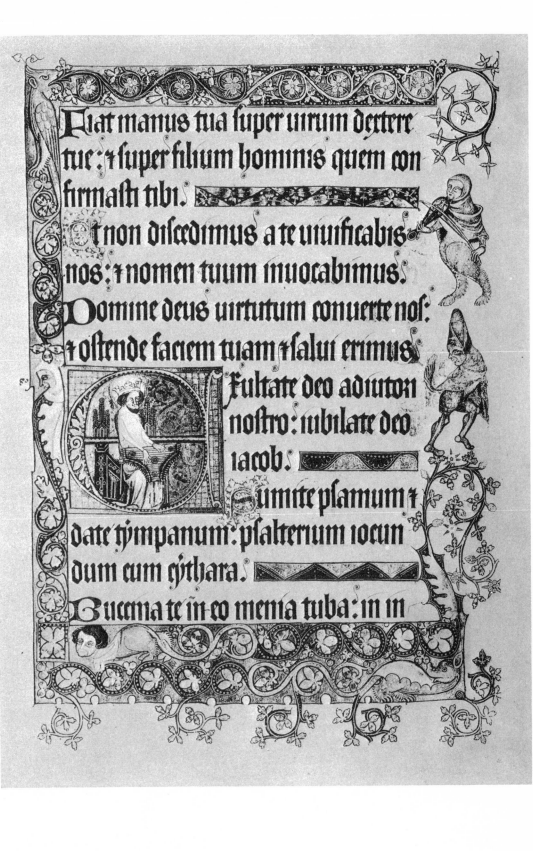

Fiat manus tua super uirum dextere
tue: ↄ super filium hominis quem con
firmasti tibi.

Et non discedimus a te uiuificabis
nos: ↄ nomen tuum inuocabimus.

Domine deus uirtutum conuerte nos:
ↄ ostende faciem tuam ↄ salui erimus.

Exultate deo adiutori
nostro: iubilate deo
iacob.

Sumite psalmum ↄ
date tympanum: psalterium iocun
dum cum cythara.

Buccinate in eo menia tuba: in in

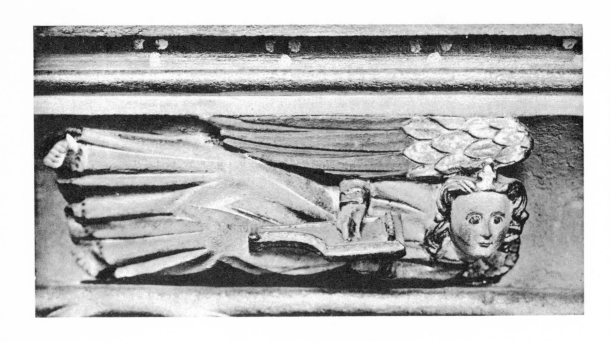

PLATE IVa

SCULPTURED FIGURE OF AN ANGEL

English, c. 1450.

THIS figure is one of a series of angels playing various musical instruments which are to be found on the canopy, added in about 1450 to the thirteenth-century effigy of Bishop Bronescombe in Exeter Cathedral (see p. 7). While no claim is made for its beauty as a piece of sculpture it is of great interest inasmuch as it is the only known English example of a psaltery of the shape on which subsequently the harpsichord and grand piano were based.

Photo by F. H. Crossley.

Exeter Cathedral.

PLATE IVb

GROTESQUE FROM THE RUTLAND PSALTER

English, c. 1250.

THE superb English psalter of Sarum use, in the possession of the Duke of Rutland at Belvoir, is one of the first manuscripts to have those grotesques and drolleries which afterwards were a characteristic feature. Drawings of the musical instruments of the period are frequently found in manuscripts of this type; and in this particular one there is a fine representation of David playing an organ with a youth blowing the bellows (figured in E. G. Millar's *La Miniature anglaise*, Pl. 80, 1926), as well as this spirited drawing of a grotesque figure plucking the strings of his psaltery with the usual plectra, which were often used instead of the fingers.

His Grace the Duke of Rutland.

85

PLATE V

PAGE FROM THE " SFORZA BOOK OF HOURS "

Italian, c. 1490.

THE superb illuminated manuscript, known as the Sforza Book of Hours and justly considered one of the finest extant examples of Italian Renaissance art, was executed for Bona of Savoy, wife of Galeazzo Maria—second Duke of Milan of the house of Sforza—and mother of Bianca Sforza, to whom she may have given it as a wedding present. One of the best sets of miniatures in the book is a beautiful series of eighteen which illustrates the Hours of the Holy Spirit; the subject of each being an angel playing on a musical instrument. The page chosen shows an angel playing on a psaltery of unusual shape. The instrument is evidently an elaborated *strumento di porco*, and has three roses in the soundboard.

The background of this miniature is crimson; the angel's wings and the crossed bands on his breast, gold; the dress, a delicate grey; the collar, green; the sleeves, pale blue.

5¼ in. by 4 in.

British Museum, London (Add. MS., 34294).

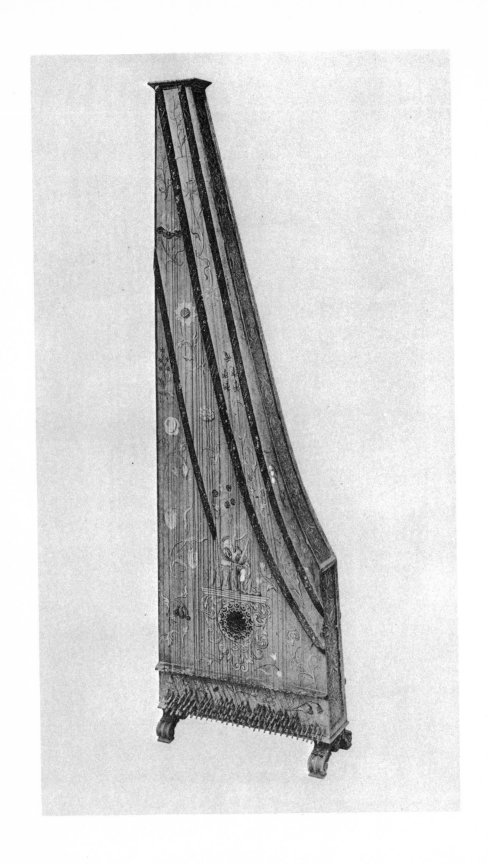

PLATE VI

DOUBLE PSALTERY

Flemish, XVIIth century.

THIS form of psaltery was of far greater popularity on the Continent than in England (see p. 7, note 4). The two soundboards of this Flemish instrument are decorated in the same style as those of the contemporary harpsichords and virginals with fruit and flowers, and are reminiscent of the borders of the Flemish illuminated manuscripts. Above the elaborate rose there is a painting of David playing the harp. The lowest notes are reinforced with octave strings—again a device copied from the keyboard instruments which had a complete set of strings of four foot tone.

Height, 5 ft. 5 in.; greatest width, 1 ft. 7 in.; depth, 3 in.

Donaldson Museum, Royal College of Music, London.

PLATE VII

CARVED IVORY COVER OF A PSALTER

Byzantine, XIIth century.

THE psalter was probably written for Melisenda, daughter of Baldwin II, King of Jerusalem, and wife of Fulk, Count of Anjou and King of Jerusalem (1131-1134). This upper cover is occupied by six circular medallions containing scenes from the life of David. In the last of these the King is seated beneath a canopy playing a dulcimer, while his four musicians also play upon harps, a rebec, and a viol. This is the earliest known representation of a dulcimer if its use by the Assyrians is disallowed (see p. 5, note 1). For a full description of this ivory see O. M. Dalton's *Catalogue of Ivory Carvings of the Christian era ... the British Museum,* 1909.

8½ in. by 5⅔ in

British Museum, London (Egerton MS., 1139).

PLATE VIII

MINIATURE FROM AN ILLUMINATED MANUSCRIPT

French, XVIth century.

THIS charming miniature from a manuscript in the Bibliothèque Nationale, entitled *Le Livre des Echecs Amoureux,* is a symbolic representation of Music. The lady seated on two swans plays a dulcimer. On the ground in front of her there is a portative organ and a recorder; to her right is a harp. In the gallery behind two choristers and three boys sing from a manuscript, while representative instruments are played by other musicians—the bag-pipes, a shawm, and the pipe and tabor.

Bibliothèque Nationale, Paris (MS. Français, 143).

PLATE IX

DULCIMER

Italian, XVIIth century.

In common with the Italian keyboard instruments this dulcimer has an outer case, which in this instance is elaborately painted, the cartouche on the inside of the lid containing a representation of Apollo and the Muses. The strings (now missing) are, as is usual in Italian dulcimers of this period, arranged in sets of five to be tuned in unison, except the lowest notes which have sets of four strings. The small hammers used for striking the strings have also disappeared. They would have been put, when not in use, in the curved hollow on the left side of the soundboard. The hitch-pins of the longest strings, some of which pass through the slit in the hollow, cannot be seen as they are fixed on the extreme outside of the instrument nearest the outer case.

Greatest width, 2 ft. 10$\frac{1}{2}$ in.; smallest width, 1 ft. 5 in.

Victoria and Albert Museum, London.

PLATE X

GOBELINS TAPESTRY PANEL

French, c. 1730.

THIS symbolic representation of Music under the title of *Le Concert* forms the subject for "April" in the set of tapestries woven by the Gobelins factory and called *Les douze Mois de Lucas*, as they are supposed to be taken from designs made by the famous Dutch artist, Lucas van Leyden. This panel depicts a *fête champêtre*, at which a lady in a rich Renaissance dress sits amongst the flowers and listens to the music made by her attendants. One of them sings and beats time, a seated girl plays the dulcimer, and a third standing by the trunk of the tree is playing the cither (see also p. 9).

Height, 13 ft. 4 in.; width, 10 ft. 4 in.

Lady Lever Art Gallery, Port Sunlight. (Reproduced by permission of the Trustees and B. T. Batsford, Ltd., from the " Catalogue of Furniture, Tapestry and Needlework of the XVIth-XIXth centuries," by P. Macquoid.)

PLATE XI A AND B

PEN AND WASH DRAWINGS

German, c. 1440.

THESE crude but vigorous drawings from a *Wunderbuch* at Weimar date from about 1440, and are, therefore, some of the earliest known graphic representations of the clavichord (Fig. *a*) and the clavicymbal, or earliest form of the harpsichord (Fig. *b*). No degree of accuracy has been reached by the artist, but the instruments are named *clavicordium* and *clavicymbalum* respectively in this interesting manuscript which contains drawings of several other instruments of the period (see A. Schultz, *Deutsches Leben im XIV und XV Jahrhundert,* 518 *ff.*, 1892). Miss K. Schlesinger, in her article on the keyboard in the *Encyclopaedia Britannica* (11th ed.), calls attention to the disposition of the keys, pointing out that one narrow additional key is let in between each pair of wider keys—an arrangement found in other early representations of the keyboard before it became chromatic some time in the fifteenth century.

Grand-Ducal Library, Weimar.

PLATE XII

CLAVICHORD

By Alessandro Trasuntino (?)

Italian, 1537.

In spite of the fact that this instrument has been extensively altered from its original construction it is illustrated because it nevertheless has most of the characteristic features of the earliest surviving clavichords (see p. 15). These are the projection of the keyboard, the arrangement of the wrest-pins in a straight line parallel with the side of the case, and the straight bridges on the soundboard instead of the more familiar but later S-shaped bridge. These features are also present in the earliest perfect example of a clavichord which is also of Italian origin, being dated 1543 (figured and described in Kinsky, pp. 25-27). In the following plate we see the gradual transition to the type of instrument generally used in the eighteenth century.

The attribution of this clavichord to the well-known Venetian instrument-maker Alessandro Trasuntino, who made the fine *clavicembalo* now in the Donaldson Museum, rests upon a highly suspicious inscription round the inside of the case. It reads as follows: *Alex. Trasontini ut osa flos florum ita hoe clavle claviluim hoc opus. 1537.* This should, of course, read *ut rosa flos florum ita hoc clavile clavilium*, etc. The keys have been arranged in an unorthodox and purely arbitrary manner. On the inside of the lid of the leather-covered case there are stamped the arms of a count of the family Gattola of Gaeta.

Length, 2 ft. 5 in.; width, 1 ft. $1\frac{3}{4}$ in.; depth, $5\frac{1}{4}$ in.

Metropolitan Museum of Art, New York.

93

PLATE XIII

CLAVICHORD

German, c. 1680.

IN this South German *gebunden* instrument the wrest-pins are still arranged parallel with the case, but the projecting keyboard and the short straight bridges of the earliest clavichords, which can be seen in the previous plate, are gone. Instead there are the recessed keyboard which probably originated in Italy about 1570, and a slightly curved bridge which later developed into the usual S-shaped bridge (see the next plate). The compass is four octaves and the forty-eight notes are obtained from twenty-three pairs of strings, the eleven lowest notes being *bundfrei* (see Stuttgart Cat., pp. 7-8, for table of the notes given to each pair of strings). The inside of the case is decorated with gold embossed paper.

Württembergisches Landesgewerbemuseum, Stuttgart.

PLATE XIV

CLAVICHORD

BY PETER HICKS

English, c. 1720.

THE fact that this is the only English clavichord known to exist perhaps helps to justify the preference for loud music traditionally ascribed to the English. Nothing is known about the maker. The use of mahogany for the case, the S-shaped bridge, and the bent line of the wrest-pins indicate that it dates from about 1720. It is fretted (*gebunden*), as the fifty-one keys, giving the usual compass at this date of four octaves and a note, C-D, act on only twenty-five pairs of strings (see Hipkins, p. 63, for a tabulated list of the actual notes played on each pair of strings in this instrument). The black naturals and white semitones also indicate its date, as the earlier clavichords usually had box-wood naturals and darker semitones.

Length, 4 ft. 1 in.; width, 14 in.; depth, $4\frac{1}{2}$ in.

Victoria and Albert Museum, London.

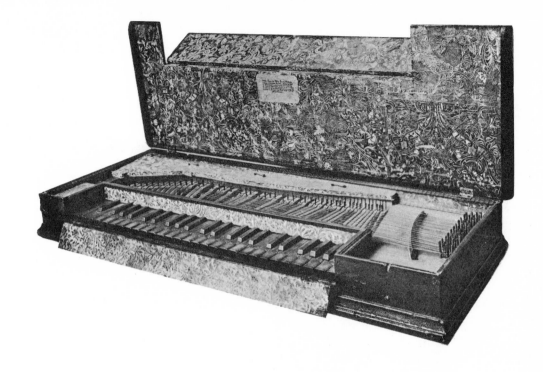

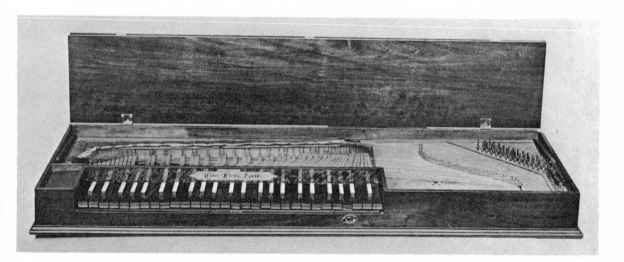

PLATE XV

CLAVICHORD

By Barthold Fritz of Brunswick

German, 1751.

THIS instrument formerly belonged to Carl Engel, who has given us many interesting details about its maker (*Musical Times,* July 1879). Fritz also made organs, harpsichords, some pianos, musical boxes, etc., and he wrote a short work on equal temperament which was published in Leipzig in 1756. He died in 1766 at the age of seventy, and his portrait, with his trade-mark below it, was engraved just after his death (see Brunswick Cat., p. 4, for reproduction). In several details of construction this clavichord is an exceptional instrument. First, the compass of five octaves and a third, F-A, is greater than that usually given to clavichords in the middle of the eighteenth century; secondly, in addition to the usual two strings tuned in unison for each note, the bottom thirty-two notes have a third string of thinner wire tuned an octave higher. The wrest-pins of these strings are put with the hitch-pins of the ordinary strings. Engel suggests that this was an attempt to copy the octave stop on the harpsichord. Thirdly, the dimensions are greater than usual and the decoration is, for a clavichord, almost lavish. The case is painted green and inside the lid is a blue monochrome painting of a stag-hunt: the naturals are of ebony, and the sharps of ivory. The latter have a design in black engraved on them. The soundboard is of usual thickness, *i.e.* one eighth of an inch, and is inscribed near the bridge *Barthold Fritz fecit Braunschweig anno 1751 Mens. Febr.*

Length, 5 ft. $10\frac{1}{2}$ in.; width, 1 ft. $10\frac{1}{2}$ in.; depth, $5\frac{5}{8}$ in.

Victoria and Albert Museum, London.

95

PLATE XVI

CLAVICHORD

By Christian Gottlob Hubert

German, 1783.

Hubert (1714-1793) was one of the foremost makers of German clavichords in the eighteenth century. By 1740 he had settled at Bayreuth and later he moved to Ansbach, where he was instrument-maker to the court, with the title *Hochfürstlich Anspach-ischer Hof-Instrumenten-Bauer*. He also made organs and pianos. Several of his instruments exist to-day: there are clavichords by him in the museums at Leipzig, Berlin, Munich, and Basle, and there is also at Leipzig one of his pianos made in the shape of an English spinet. In a short biography Kinsky (p. 235) quotes a passage from Gerber's *Lexikon der Tonkünstler*, 1790, in which it is stated that " his instruments comprising Clavichords, Harpsichords and Pianofortes, after original and improved designs, were much sought after, expensive, and to some extent exported to France, England, and Holland." The instrument in this plate—of plainer appearance than most of his surviving clavichords which are elaborately decorated in rococo style—is of a compass of four and a half octaves, C-G. The naturals, with arcaded fronts, are of black ebony and the semitones are of ivory. The stand containing two drawers is a later reconstruction.

Length, 4 ft. 7½ in.; width, 1 ft. 2½ in.; depth (without stand), 7½ in.

Messrs. Rushworth & Dreaper, Liverpool.

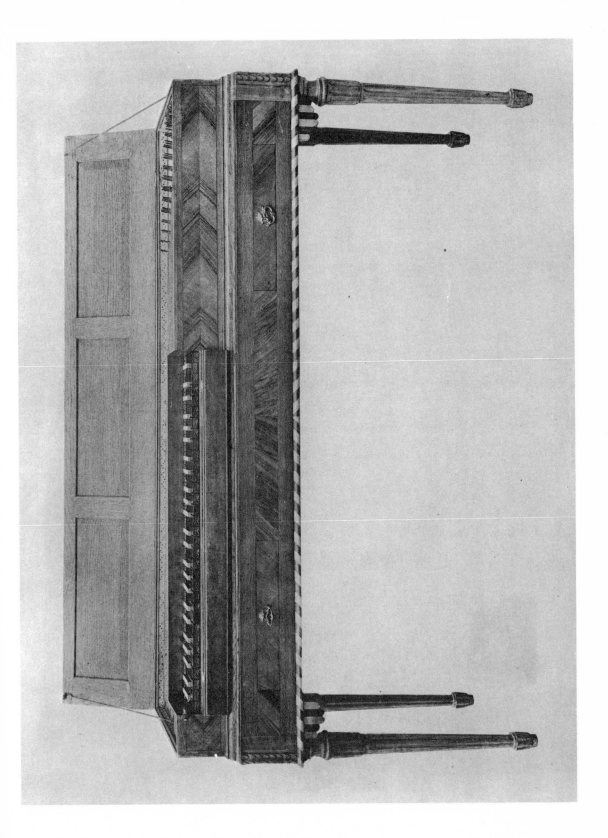

PLATE XVII

CLAVICHORD

By Arnold Dolmetsch

English, 1924

This modern instrument is distinguished by its just proportions, restrained ornamentation, and fine craftsmanship. It is made of Italian walnut. In design it is similar to the early square pianos and clavichords of the eighteenth century, and it has the traditional arcaded key-fronts, black naturals and white sharps, small box on the left of the keyboard for spare strings and tuning-key, and compass of four octaves and a note, C-D. The inscription on the inside of the lid is of special significance as the instrument was given by a body of admirers to Mr. Robert Bridges, Poet Laureate.

The late Mr. Robert Bridges.

PLATE XVIII

VIRGINAL

Flemish, 1568.

MOST of the Netherlandish virginals were made to rest on a stand or simply on a table, and examples of this type made in faithful representation of a coffer are rare. The case of this instrument, which has been carefully restored, is of walnut, finely carved with trophies of arms and musical instruments. The inside of the lid, of which the ground is painted blue, is decorated with a medallion in the centre of Orpheus charming the beasts, gilt carved strapwork and corner-pieces, and Latin mottoes also in gold, which the Flemish craftsmen so often inscribed on their instruments. The falling front and the jack-rail are similarly inscribed in gold. The outside of the lid is carved with floral scrollwork and an oval medallion in the centre, which contains the arms of William, called Le Riche, Duke of Cleves, Berg, and Jülich (b. 1516, d. 1592). The ends are each carved with a cartouche containing an animal's head in high relief holding an iron ring in its mouth (see p. 23).

The keys are of boxwood and the unusual compass of three octaves and a sixth, A-F, would be extended by short octave down to G or F, making four octaves. The wrest-pins are arranged in the V formation often adopted by Flemish craftsmen. This virginal was formerly in the collection of M. Terme of Liège who lent it to the Exposition Nationale Belge held at Brussels in 1880 (see *L'art ancien à l'Exposition nationale belge*, p. 304, 1882).

Length, 5 ft. 7 in.; width, 2 ft. 4 in.; height, 16 in.

Victoria and Albert Museum, London.

98

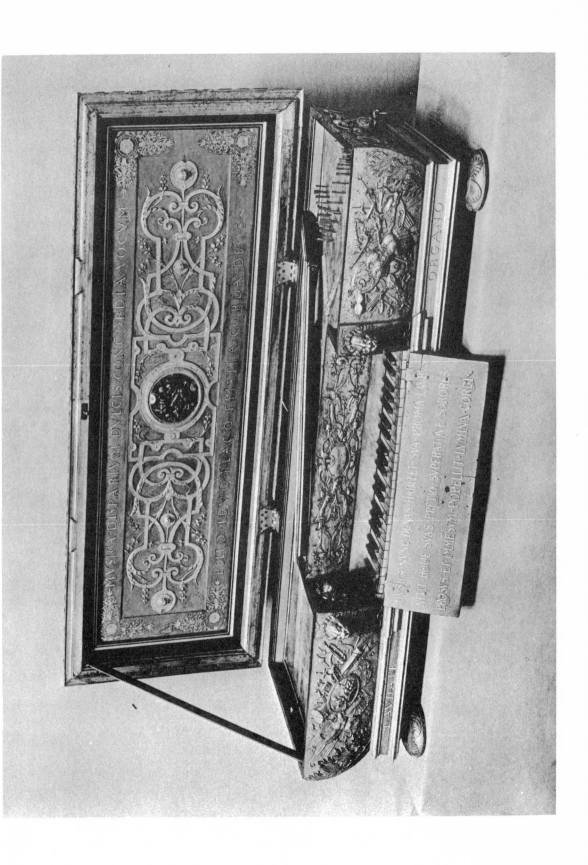

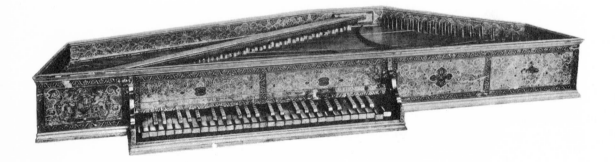

PLATE XIX

SPINET

Italian, c. 1570.

THIS spinet of unusually fine workmanship is traditionally stated to have belonged to Queen Elizabeth whose arms and device it bears. It has always been known as " Queen Elizabeth's Virginal " in accordance with the English custom of calling all the domestic keyboard instruments " virginals " before the Restoration. The shape of the case, the materials used, and the style of decoration at once proclaim it to be a typical hexagonal Italian spinet of the best period. It is made of cypress wood and has a compass of four octaves and a fourth with short octave, and the usual one string to each note. The thirty naturals are mounted with ebony and the key-fronts have a stamped gilt ornamentation. The twenty sharps are inlaid with silver, ivory, and various woods. The case is elaborately decorated with arabesques painted in red and blue on a gold ground which form panels on the front. The usual outer case, which has also been preserved, is covered with crimson Genoese velvet and lined with yellow tabby silk. The three gilt lockplates fitted to it are finely engraved, and the inside of the rising flap is ornamented with flowers and tendrils in gold on a gold-sprinkled black ground.

The striking resemblance between this instrument and a spinet now in the Leipzig University collection, made by Benedetto Floriani of Venice in 1571 (figured in Kinsky, p. 58), makes the conjecture that they were both made by this craftsman not unreasonable. In both there is a strong oriental influence in the design of the decoration which is similarly divided into panels on the front, and the cases are identical in shape. These points of resemblance tend to discount the claim that this instrument was decorated in England (*Dict. English Furniture*, iii, Pl. i), which is based on the presence of the royal arms of Elizabeth on the panel on the left of the keyboard and her device of a crowned falcon on the panel to the right. There is no evidence to prove that the Italian instruments, which were so often imported at this time, were sent " naked " to be decorated in England. The device of the falcon—on a tree stump eradicated, a falcon argent crowned, and holding in its right claw a sceptre, or—has sometimes been cited as proof that the spinet came to Elizabeth from her mother, Anne Boleyn, who used this badge. But Elizabeth continued to use the badge of her mother, and the date of the instrument makes this impossible. From a description of this spinet in the *Gentleman's Magazine*, 1815, pt. i, p. 593, its history is known from before 1800, when it belonged to Lord Chichester of Fisherwick. It is mentioned in the description of this seat in S. Shaw's *Hist. and Antiq. of Staffordshire*, i, p. 369, 1798, where the author says " it is in shape and size much like a spinnet but opens on the opposite side, and then resembles a common piano forte "!

Case: height, 5 ft. 5 in.; width, 1 ft. 11 in.; depth, 8½ in.
Spinet: length, 5 ft.; width, 16 in.; depth, 7 in.

Victoria and Albert Museum, London.

99

PLATE XX

SPINET

BY ANNIBALE ROSSO OF MILAN

Italian, 1577.

THIS exceptional instrument is ornamented with ivory and nearly two thousand precious and semi-precious stones, *e.g.* pearls, emeralds, rubies, sapphires, turquoises, amethysts, jaspars, agates, garnets, etc. (see Engel, p. 272, for full list). It has the usual one string to each note and the usual compass of four octaves and a fifth with short octave. The nameboard is inscribed *Anniballis De Roxis Mediolanensis MDLXXVII*. This lavish and costly decoration, which would certainly have an ill effect on the tone, is doubtless explained by the fact that the instrument was made for a member of the wealthy Milanese family of Trivulzio, whose collections of art objects were famed for their magnificence. We learn this from a passage—discovered by Engel—in P. Morigi's *La Nobilta di Milano*, p. 289, 1595, in which the great reputation won by the maker of this spinet is also recorded:

> Annibale Rosso was worthy of praise for having been the first maker to modernize spinets into that shape in which we see them to-day. This brilliant craftsman made amongst his other works a spinet of rare beauty and quality with keys entirely of precious stones, and with the most choice ornaments, which was sold for five hundred crowns, and is in the possession of the learned, most distinguished, and illustrious Signor Carlo Trivulzio. And Ferrante his son in every way follows in his father's footsteps, making fresh improvements on spinets for which he is much commended.

There can be little doubt that this refers to the spinet illustrated here. The word *clavicordo* is used in the Italian, but this was a common if confusing practice, and it is not to be translated clavichord for which *manicordo* was employed (see p. 14). All the surviving examples of Rosso's work are of very high quality, and the less ornate instruments are usually decorated with superbly carved wooden figures and strapwork, and with a most intricate rose on the soundboard (Pl. XXIIIA). The alteration in the shape of his instruments referred to in the passage quoted is probably the recessing of the keyboard, which is absent from spinets and clavichords made by other Italian craftsmen at this period, *e.g.* the spinet associated with Queen Elizabeth (Pl. XIX). Rosso was working from about 1550 and he died between 1577 and 1595. His son Ferrante was not so accomplished a craftsman if we can judge him from a spinet made by him which is now in the Museo Civico, Turin (figured in a catalogue of plates, No. 38, published by the Museum in 1905).

Length, 4 ft. 10 in.; width, 1 ft. 10 in.; depth, $11\frac{1}{4}$ in.

Victoria and Albert Museum, London.

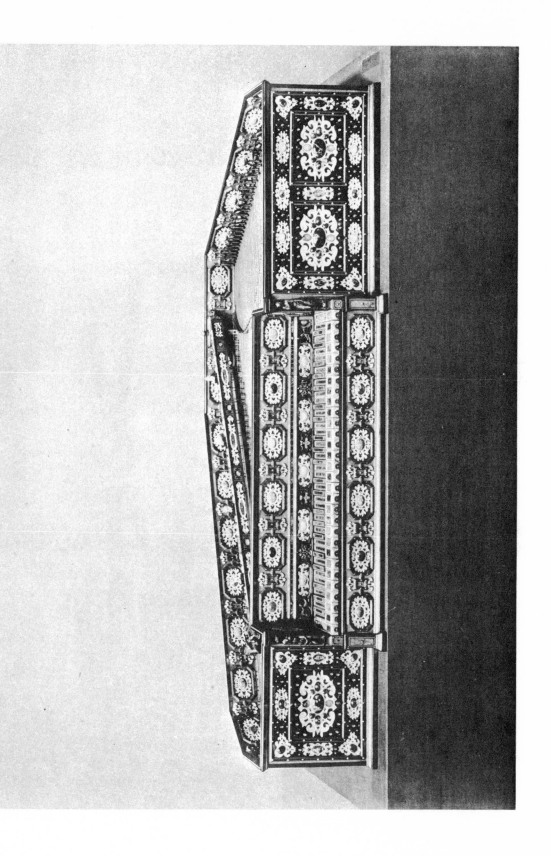

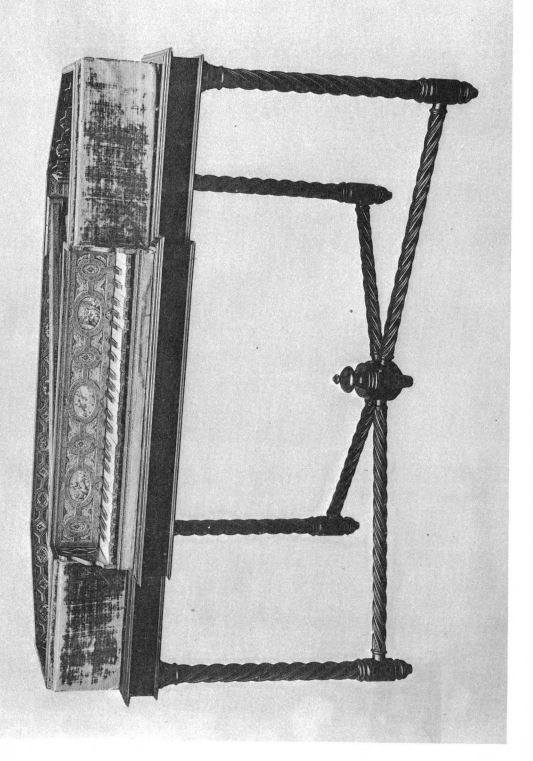

PLATE XXI

SPINET

By Giovanni Celestini of Venice

Italian, 1593.

THIS is one of the most elaborate specimens of an Italian poly-gonal spinet. Its original outer case of faded crimson Genoese velvet has doubtless helped to preserve the elaborate decoration in gilt and colours on the interior of the case and the nameboard. The raised strapwork forms alternate diamond and oval com-partments round the inside of the case, and three larger ovals on the nameboard which contain miniatures of Orpheus, Apollo, and Pan, etc., painted on mother-of-pearl and ivory. The jack-rail is inscribed JOANNIS CELESTINI VENETI MDXCIII. Compass, four octaves and a fifth—by short octave, B-F. The stand is modern.

In the *Daily Journal* of 16th May 1724, an announcement of a sale of a collection of instruments belonging to William Corbett, the violinist and composer, mentions " two fine-toned Cyprus Spinnets, one of Celestini, and the other of Donatus Undeus." The word " Cyprus " does not refer to a Cyprian provenance, but to the fact that they were made—in common with most Italian spinets—of *cypress* wood. An unusual instrument by this maker described as an *arci-spineta*, *i.e.* a virginal with an elong-ated soundboard, is in the Musée Instrumental at Brussels (Catalogue, No. 1590).

Length, 4 ft. 9 in.; width, 16½ in.; depth, 7¼ in.

Donaldson Museum, Royal College of Music, London.

PLATE XXII

OCTAVE SPINET

Italian, late XVIth century.

THE pitch of the *ottavina* was an octave higher than was indicated by the notation, while the notes of the *mezza spinetta* were a fifth higher (see p. 26). This example being Italian is preserved in the usual outer case, which in this instance is elaborately painted. The inside of the lid is decorated with a ship in full sail, marine deities, dancing figures, and musical trophies, which are attributed to Federigo Zucchero. But there is no evidence to support this conjecture. The nameboard is finely ornamented with a row of figures etched in gold. The compass is three octaves and a sixth, E-C, and there is only one string for each note. These instruments of a higher pitch and smaller size were not made for long as the octave string was soon incorporated into the mechanism of the harpsichord by the use of stops.

Length, 2 ft. $3\frac{1}{8}$ in.; width, 17 in.

Victoria and Albert Museum, London.

PLATE XXIII

(a) ROSE IN THE SOUND-HOLE OF A SPINET MADE BY ANNIBALE ROSSO

Italian, 1555.

(b) ROSE WITH THE DEVICE OF HANS RUCKERS, THE ELDER, IN A HARPSICHORD

Flemish, 1612.

THE sound-hole with an ornamental rose, or knot, is found in nearly all keyboard instruments before the eighteenth century, except the clavichord; and then it was still retained by some makers. We must note the analogy from the psaltery, lute, guitar, and other stringed instruments which sometimes had as many as three sound-holes. In these instruments, as in the violin, the sound-hole is essential as it controls the volume of vibrating air within the body of the instrument and therefore the tone. In the keyboard instruments, on the other hand, the soundboard—acting in this case as the lid of a *closed* sound-chest—is of a so much greater area that it suffices to amplify the vibration of the strings, and a sound-hole is unnecessary. In both types of instrument the vibrations are conveyed to the sound-chest, or body of the instrument, by means of the bridge.

The rose in the sound-hole was often used as an opportunity for decorative ingenuity by instrument-makers. Sometimes it took the form of intricately carved Gothic tracery, or an elaborate geometric design as in this rose from one of Annibale Rosso's spinets (a): or craftsmen sometimes used it as a method of signing their work by inventing a trade-mark to which they added their name or initials. Each of the Ruckers family had his own device, which is in several instances the only means of attributing an instrument to its proper source. They are all engraved in Grove (article *Ruckers*). That of Hans the elder—an angel seated playing a harp—is illustrated here (b): it is encircled with paintings on the soundboard in the usual Flemish manner. His son Hans (usually known as Jean) had three roses in which the figure faced to the left front and right, respectively, but he used the initials I.R. and he signed himself Joannes to avoid confusion. Andreas also used a device similar to that of his father with the initials A.R.

Of the two famous English makers of the eighteenth century, Kirkman and Shudi, only the former retained the sound-hole. He chose as a device King David playing the harp between the initials I.K.

(a) *Victoria and Albert Museum, London.*
(b) *His Majesty The King.*

103

PLATE XXIV

TITLE-PAGE OF *PARTHENIA*

English, 1611.

THIS was the first collection of virginal music to be printed from engraved plates. The title-page reproduced here reads as follows:

Parthenia or The Maydenhead of the first musicke that ever was printed for the Virginalls. Composed by three famous Masters: William Byrd, Dr. John Bull, & Orlando Gibbons, Gentilmen of his Maties most Illustrious Chappell. Dedicated to all the Maisters and Louers of Musick. Ingrauen by William Hole for Dorethie Euans. Cum Priuilegio. Printed at London by G: Lowe and are to be soulde at his howse in Loathberry.

The work contains twenty-one pieces on six-line staves, of which eight are by Byrd, seven by Bull, and six by Gibbons. As a collection of virginal music it does not equal in importance the more famous manuscript books such as the Fitzwilliam Virginal Book and Lady Nevill's book (see Grove, article *Virginal Music*). There are copies of the first edition of *Parthenia*, which was published in 1611, in the British Museum, the Bodleian Library, the Royal College of Music, and the Henry E. Huntington Library.

The title-page is also engraved with a three-quarter length representation of a lady playing the virginals. The drawing of the instrument, however, is far from accurate; *e.g.* there are no accidentals. It is also interesting to note that contrary to the accepted custom—unless this is also evidence of the engraver's ignorance—the player is using her thumb. This recalls the astonishing proficiency of technique required for this virginal music which Sir W. H. Hadow comments upon in his essay on Byrd (*Collected Essays*, p. 51, 1928):

the system which continued in use as late as Purcell allows the thumb and little finger only at the beginning and end of a two-octave scale. All the other notes are struck by the third and fourth fingers in ascending movement and in descending by the third and second. Even our masters of technical proficiency might look upon these restrictions with some misgiving.

Royal College of Music, London.

PARTHENIA

or

THE MAYDENHEAD

of the first musicke that

ever was printed for the VIRGINALLS ..

COMPOSED

By three famous Masters: William Byrd. D: John Bull, & Orlando Gibbons.
Gentilmen of his Ma:tie: most Illustrious Chappell.
Dedicated to all the Masters and Lovers of Musick

Ingrauen
by William Hole.
for
DORETHIE EVANS
Cum
Priuilegio.

Printed at LONDON by G: Lowe and are to be soulde
at his howse in Loathberry.

PLATE XXV

VIRGINAL

By Andreas Ruckers, the Elder

Flemish, 1620.

THIS virginal may be said to represent the Ruckers' ordinary standard workmanship, for it was only to a special order or for a wealthy and distinguished patron that the lids were painted. The block-printed yellow papers with their black Renaissance designs were much used by them to cover the cases, and they almost invariably inscribed a latin motto—often a verse from a psalm—on the lid when it was not painted. The soundboard is painted with flowers, sprays of foliage, birds, and insects, and bears the date 1620. The signature is on the jack-rail, as in most of the instruments by this family, who seldom signed their names on the board above the keys: it reads *Andreas Ruckers me fecit Antwerpiae.* The wrest-pins are set in the V-shaped formation usually adopted in these virginals. In one thing this instrument is unusual, for the usual compass of four octaves is not obtained by short octave but is actually extended to the full chromatic scale. It must also be noted that the disposition of the jacks in a diagonal line across the soundboard made it possible for the plucking point of each string to be exactly at the middle point of its vibrating length. The tone was therefore remarkably clear and pure. The lay-out of the soundboard of a virginal is clearly seen in the next plate.

Length, 5 ft. 8 in.; width, 1 ft. $7\frac{1}{2}$ in.

Musée Instrumental du Conservatoire, Brussels.

PLATE XXVI

DOUBLE VIRGINAL

BY JEAN RUCKERS

Flemish, 1623.

THE small octave instrument is here seen projecting from the case of the virginal to which it belongs. It can be removed and placed on a table for use by a second performer (see p. 27). Both instruments are signed on the jack-rail JOANNES RUCKERS ME FECIT, and this maker's rose can be seen in the two sound-holes. The soundboards are painted with flowers in the traditional Flemish style and are decorated with *pointillé* ornaments similar to those which bookbinders were beginning to use at this date.

Sometimes the recess for the octave instrument was on the right of the keyboard.

There are only six other double virginals known to exist. To the list of them in Grove (see vol. iv, p. 472) must be added one by Louis Grauwels, which is dated 1600. It is now in the Metropolitan Museum, New York. There was a family of craftsmen of this name in Antwerp, and Louis was probably the son of Hans Grauwels, who became a master of the Guild of St. Luke in 1579, and who has left a specimen of his work in a fine virginal now in the Musée Instrumental at Brussels.

The oldest surviving Ruckers instrument is a double virginal dated 1581 which is also in the Metropolitan Museum, New York (see the museum *Bulletin,* Feb. 1930).

Length, 5 ft. 8 in.; width, 1 ft. 8 in.

MM. M. & A. Salomon.

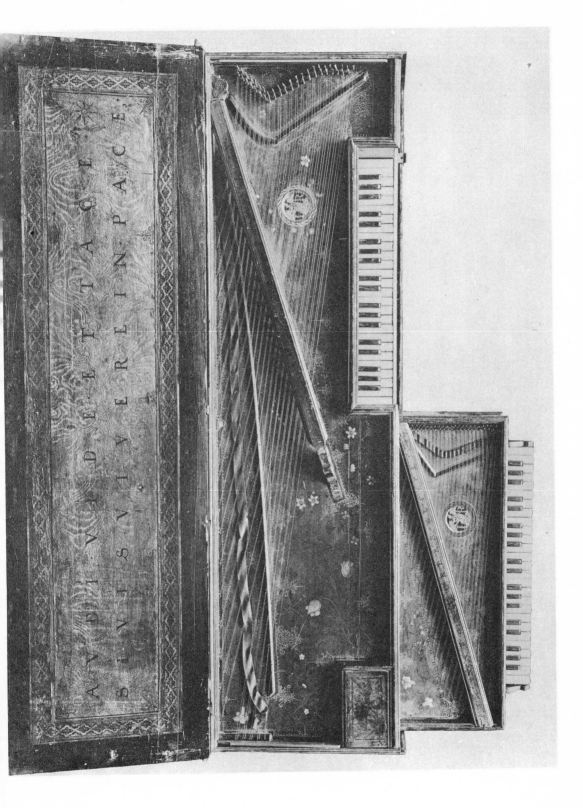

PLATE XXVII

PAINTING

By Jan Vermeer of Delft

Dutch, second half of the XVIIth century.

This famous painting at Windsor Castle well illustrates the love of the Dutch genre painters for musical scenes. The young woman stands before a virginal receiving a lesson. We must notice the faithful representation of the instrument which is decorated with the printed papers often used by the Ruckers family. Indeed, the virginal by Andreas Ruckers, illustrated in Pl. XXV is decorated with the same papers. In one of Vermeer's two other pictures in the National Gallery, with representations of virginals, the player is also standing in front of the instrument. Virginals, and less often harpsichords, are depicted in numerous other canvases by Metsu, Gerard Dou, Steen, Ochtervelt, Molenaer and others, and in every case the player is a woman. This seems to leave the origin of the name *virginal* beyond doubt. Male performers are usually shown with the lute and viola da gamba.

29 in. by 25½ in.

By the gracious permission of His Majesty the King.

PLATE XXVIII

VIRGINAL

By John Loosemoore

English, 1655.

THIS is a typical specimen of the English virginal of the seventeenth century. The rectangular oak case, with its domed lid, the boxwood naturals and ebony sharps, the painting inside the lid (in this case of a hunting scene, a sea fight, and Adam and Eve), the embossed and gilt pasteboard decoration, and the paintings of flowers and fruits on the soundboard in the Flemish manner, are all characteristic features of these instruments. The stand is original. By short octave the compass is four octaves and a fifth, G-D. John Loosemoore was also renowned as an organ-builder, and in 1665 he built the organ in Exeter Cathedral. Other famous makers of the English virginal were Adam Leversidge, Stephen Keene, and Thomas and James White.

Length, 5 ft. 8½ in.; width, 1 ft. 8½ in.; height, 3 ft. 6 in.

Victoria and Albert Museum, London.

PLATE XXIX

SPINET

BY JOHN PLAYER

English, c. 1680.

FROM the use of oak for the case and stand, and from the size of the case this must be classed as one of the first of the three different types of English spinet described on page 30. The apparent compass of four octaves and two notes is extended by short octave to four octaves and a fourth, G-C. The two bottom sharps are split—a device consistent with the short octave system of this period which includes the chromatic notes which are played by the back halves (see p. 31). The split sharp, which has been mistaken by some writers as an attempt to obtain quarter tones, is confined to instruments of the last half of the seventeenth century and first twenty years of the eighteenth, by which time the introduction of equal temperament removed the necessity for any short octave system.

John Player also made harpsichords, but a specimen has not survived so far as is known.

Length, 4 ft. 10 in.; greatest width, 1 ft. 6½ in.; depth, 6½ in.

Victoria and Albert Museum, London.

PLATE XXX

SPINET

By Benjamin Slade

English, 1700.

A GREATER profusion of marquetry is found on this decorative spinet than was usual on English instruments, the nameboard and inside of the case being covered with inlay of a bird pattern, which was popular at this date. The jack-rail is inscribed *Benjamin Slade faciebat 1700.* No other record of this maker has been found. Here again the two bottom sharps are split, giving a chromatic scale of four octaves and a fifth, G-D. The sharps throughout are inlaid with strips of dark wood in the style always used by the Hitchcocks.

Photo by courtesy of Messrs. Edwards, Regent Street, London.

PLATE XXXI

SPINET

BY JOSEPH HARRIS

English, 1757.

THIS is a fine example of the English spinet in its most fully developed form. The compass of five octaves is usual at this period. The front of the nameboard is inscribed in gold JOSEPH HARRIS, LONDON, MDCCLVII, and on the back of it a piece of parchment is pasted bearing the following inscription in a contemporary hand: " This is not one of my Com̄on Instruments But the Best Ton'd I Ever made. Joseph Harris. London 1756." The maker's claim that it is a special instrument is supported by the presence of two stops which are very seldom found on spinets, although they were a usual feature of the contemporary harpsichords: the strings are as usual stretched in pairs, and one of each pair is muted by the stop regulated at the left of the nameboard, and the other by the one on the right. Both of these buff stops must therefore be used together. The case is of figured walnut inlaid with lines of sycamore, and the stand is of mahogany, with turned balusters, supported on cabriole legs with claw-and-ball feet.

Joseph Harris and his son John were both well known instrument makers. The latter went to Boston, Mass., in 1768, and an interesting extract from the *Boston Gazette*, 18th September 1769 (quoted by Dow, p. 301), claims the first spinet to be made in America to have been his work: " It is with pleasure that we inform the Public, That a few days since was shipped for Newport, a very curious Spinnet, being the first ever made in America, the performance of the ingenious Mr. John Harris, of Boston (Son of the late Mr. Joseph Harris of London, Harpsichord and Spinnet Maker), and in every respect does Honour to that Artist."

Length, 6 ft. 4 in.; greatest width, 2 ft.; height, 2 ft. 9 in.

Mr. B. Coppinger Prichard. Exhibited at the Burlington Fine Arts Club, Winter Exhibition, 1927-28.

PLATE XXXII

SPINET

By Samuel Blythe

Made in Salem, Massachusetts, 1789.

THE history of the keyboard instruments in America up to the third quarter of the eighteenth century is chiefly a record of their importation from Europe, and even then it seems that the craftsmen were usually emigrants. We learn from the references quoted by Dow and E. Singleton (*The furniture of our forefathers,* 2 vols., 1901) that virginals were as popular in New England as in the Mother Country, and that in New York, Boston, and other towns, spinets and harpsichords frequently appeared in the sale room. The instruments of English makers seem to have been especially favoured. George Washington is known to have purchased a harpsichord from Plenius of London for use at Mount Vernon, and Benjamin Franklin wrote in 1758 to his wife about his quest for a good harpsichord when he was in London.

The spinet reproduced here was made in 1789, and its resemblance to the English spinet is immediately apparent. It has been described as the first made in the country, but the advertisement from the *Boston Gazette* of 1769, quoted on the preceding page, invalidates this claim. Samuel Blythe—we are told by H. W. Belknap, *Artists and craftsmen of Essex county,* p. 29, 1927— was baptized in 1744 and died in 1795. He made most sorts of stringed instruments in his shop at Salem.

Essex Institute Museum, Salem, Mass.

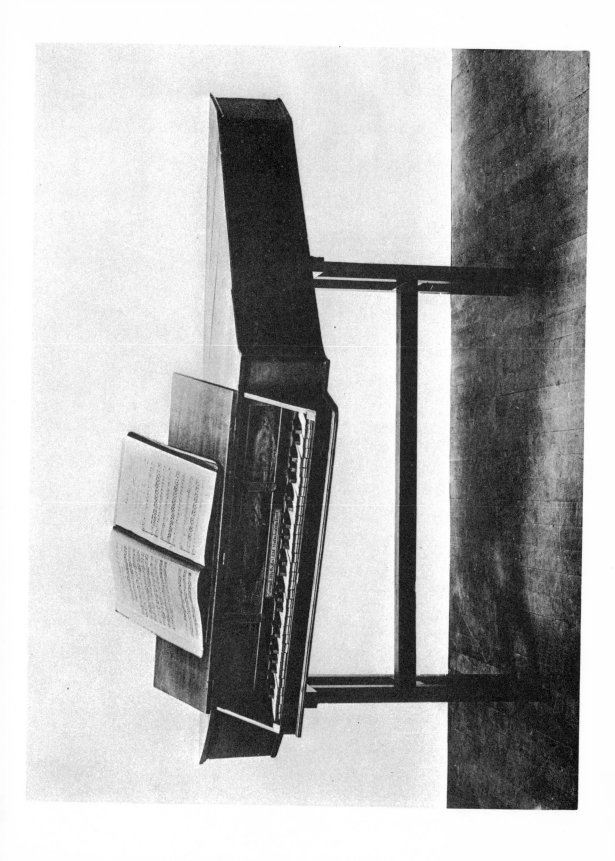

PLATE XXXIII

UPRIGHT HARPSICHORD (CLAVICYTHERIUM)

North Italian, second half of XVth century.

THE earliest surviving example of a *clavicytherium*, which is reproduced in this plate, is probably of North Italian origin (see also p. 39). There is one string to each note and the jacks, moving horizontally instead of vertically as usual, are returned to their original position when the keys are released by small steel springs. The early date of the instrument can be gauged by the remains of original plectra of metal, which preceded quill and leather, the boxwood keys, the compass of three octaves and a minor third, and the general style of decoration on the soundboard. The last is unusual and its fragmentary condition makes it difficult to reconstruct the original scene: the rock in relief with a winding path perhaps suggests the subject of St. George and the Dragon which was so popular with North Italian and South German craftsmen at this period. Others consider it to have been a Calvary. A piece of paper pasted over a split in the inside of the back was discovered by Hipkins (p. 75) to be a fragment of a lease or agreement contracted at Ulm. One of the sound-holes is decorated with a miniature Gothic window instead of the more usual circular ornament. The painting of Truth on the lid of the case and the painted stand are of later date.

Another early *clavicytherium* of great interest is in the Leipzig University collection (Kinsky, p. 85). In this instrument the jacks are arranged diagonally and the soundboard is made up from two psalteries joined together. The fact that there are two keyboards is of great significance as the instrument dates from the first half of the sixteenth century. The attribution of this constructional improvement to Hans Ruckers the elder (see p. 36), supported by many musical historians, is therefore no longer acceptable. Several seventeenth-century specimens have survived, notably one in the Crosby Brown collection in the Metropolitan Museum, New York, which is enclosed in an oblong case (Grove, Pl. xix) and resembles the later " bookcase " piano.

Height, 4 ft. 10½ in.; greatest width, 2 ft. 3 in.; depth, 11 in. at base, diminishing to 5⅝ in. at top.

Stand: height, 2 ft.; width, 2 ft. 11 in.

Donaldson Museum, Royal College of Music, London.

PLATE XXXIV

HARPSICHORD

By Geronimo di Bologna

Rome, 1521.

THE interest attached to this Roman *clavicembalo* for being the oldest known harpsichord in existence is enhanced by the preservation of the original boxwood keys with arcaded fronts, and by its good condition. This is doubtless due to the survival of the outer case which is covered on the outside with leather, very finely stamped and gilt, and on the inside with the original green velvet. These outer cases were invariably made by the Italian craftsmen, both for their harpsichords and the smaller spinets. The nameboard is signed by the maker *Hieronymus Bononiensis faciebat Romae MDXXI*, and there is also the following neat elegiac couplet:

Aspicite ut trahitur suavi modulamine vocis
Quicquid habent aer sidera terra fretum.

The arms of the family for which the instrument was made, which cannot at present be identified, are painted on the nameboard at both ends. The compass of three octaves and a seventh, E-D, is one note short of that usually found on the early *clavicembali, i.e.* four octaves, C-C. There is almost certainly some arrangement of short octave, but it is difficult to ascertain the actual disposition of the last octave.

Length, 6 ft. 3 in.; width, 2 ft. $7\frac{1}{2}$ in.

Victoria and Albert Museum, London.

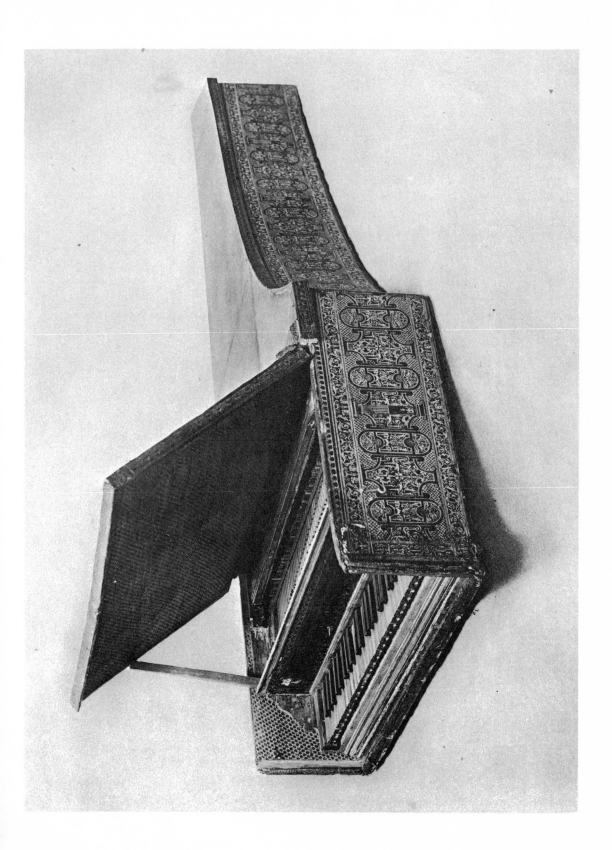

PLATE XXXV

HARPSICHORD

By Giovanni Antonio Baffo

Venice, 1574.

BAFFO was a Venetian instrument-maker of repute whose name, in common with those of other famous makers, was forged on instruments of inferior quality and later date. His period of working was of exceptional length, for there is a harpsichord in the collection at the Museum für Kunst und Industrie, Vienna, dated 1523, while another at the Conservatoire, Paris, is dated 1579. He made lutes and other stringed instruments as well as keyboard instruments. The surviving examples of his work are distinguished by craftsmanship of a high order as we can see from the harpsichord illustrated here. The case is decorated with an elaborate strapwork inlay, and with gilt arabesques and small studs of ivory. The nameboard is inscribed *Ioanes Antonius Baffo Venetus MDLXXIIII.* It has the usual compass of *clavicembali* of this period, *viz.* four octaves and a fourth, C-F, to be extended by short octave; and it has the leather plectra favoured by the Italian craftsmen instead of crow quill, although they are probably not the original plectra. There are two strings to each note. The usual outer protecting case, with the battens so often found on instruments of Italian workmanship, has also been preserved. It is decorated on the outside with boldly painted swags of flowers, and on the inside of the lid with characteristic Renaissance ornaments, including a representation of Apollo and the Muses.

Length, 7 ft. 4 in.; width, 3 ft.; depth, 9½ in.

Victoria and Albert Museum, London.

PLATE XXXVI

ORGAN-HARPSICHORD (CLAVIORGANUM)
By Ludovic Theewes

English, 1579.

THE combination of a harpsichord and a small positive organ, unsatisfactory though it may seem, was probably only one more attempt on the part of musicians to obtain variety and duration of tone, the lack of which was the great disadvantage of the plucked string action which craftsmen were always striving to remedy. There were usually three sets of pipes laid horizontally in a rectangular case on top of which the harpsichord was placed. The bellows were worked by means of a pedal or *genouillère* either by the player or by a second person who stood at the opposite end of the instrument. The pallets were controlled by the keys of the harpsichord, which also performed their usual function of moving the jacks. By the means of stops the two instruments could be played separately or together, and also the various registers of each instrument could be put in or out of action at will.

The exact provenance of this example—the earliest now in existence—has been the subject of much speculation, as Theewes is known to have been admitted to the Guild of St. Luke at Antwerp in 1558, and yet the instrument was made in 1579 for an English patron, and was certainly decorated in England. However, the discovery of the maker's migration to and residence in England (see p. 29) now fixes its origin. The case is panelled and finely painted with strapwork and other ornaments, and the lid of the harpsichord with the subject of Orpheus charming the beasts. On the long side of the organ case are the arms of Hoby and Carey, being those of Sir Edward Hoby, of Bisham, Berks, and of his wife Margaret, daughter of Henry Carey, 1st Baron Hunsdon, whom we have already met in connection with the delightful incident of Queen Elizabeth surprised at her virginal, told by Sir James Melville (p. 25). They were married in 1582 and Margaret Hoby died in 1605, so the case must have been decorated between those years (see *The Herald and Genealogist*, iv, pp. 397, 398, 1867). The oaken case of the harpsichord, once covered with leather stamped in blind and gilt, is another indication of English origin and bears the maker's inscription, *Lodowicus Theewes me fesit* 1579. There are two unison strings and one octave, and the sole remaining key shows that the accidentals were inlaid with two slips of dark wood. The organ once had five stops of both wood and metal, but only one oaken pipe now remains. For many years this instrument was in the chapel at Ightham Mote, near Sevenoaks.

Harpsichord: length, 7 ft.; width, 2 ft. 11 in.; depth, 9 in.
Organ: length, 7 ft. 7 in.; width, 3 ft. 4 in.; height, 3 ft. 5 in.

Victoria and Albert Museum, London.

PLATE XXXVII

HARPSICHORD WITH OCTAVE SPINET
By Jean Ruckers

Flemish, early XVIIth century.

INSTRUMENTS of this construction—a harpsichord with an octave instrument built into the bent side—are extremely rare. Another made by Jean Ruckers is in the Hochschule für Musik at Berlin (Sachs, Catalogue, Pl. vi); and there is one made by Hans Ruckers in 1594 in the Schloss Museum, Berlin (see list in Grove, No. A 5). An example dating from the eighteenth century, now preserved in the Plantin Museum, Antwerp, was made at Roermond: it is inscribed *Joannes Josephus Coenen presbyter et organista cathedralis me fecit Ruraemondae A° 1735.*

There can be no doubt as to the origin of the instrument before us as, although it is unsigned, both the harpsichord and the octave spinet have in their sound-holes the Ruckers device and the initials I.R. for Jean Ruckers. The block printed papers often found on their instruments are also used. The lid is painted with a copy of the version of Apollo and the Muses by Martin de Vos (d. 1603), a painter of the Antwerp school.

It is interesting to see instead of the usual brass knobs on the nameboard, the original slides, by which the four stops in this instrument were worked. They project through the side of the case, and holes are pierced in them through which cords can be passed for their manipulation. The harpsichord has three strings to each note—two unisons and an octave—and the octave instrument only one. The compass of the former is four octaves and note; and that of the latter is four octaves, C-C, of which the lowest is short.

Length, 7 ft. 3 in.; width, 2 ft. 8 in.

Musée Instrumental du Conservatoire Royal, Brussels.

PLATE XXXVIII

WOOD-ENGRAVING OF A " GEIGENWERK "

German, 1620.

THIS is taken from the famous *Theatrum instrumentorum* by Praetorius. It represents a harpsichord, the strings of which were acted upon by rosined parchment wheels which were set in motion by the treadle below the keyboard (see also p. 39). Praetorius describes it in his *Organographia,* cap. xliv, as being the invention of Hans Haiden, organist of St. Sebald in Nuremberg, who called it the *Nürmbergische Geigenwerck* or *Geigen-Clavicymbel.* A Spanish instrument of this type of approximately the same date has survived and is described in the next plate. Numerous attempts were made in a similar direction, especially in Germany, to construct a satisfactory keyboard instrument, the tones of which could be sustained by an action of this kind, right up to the end of the eighteenth century, when the perfection of the piano removed the necessity for it. These are listed and described by Kinsky (p. 383).

The *Theatrum instrumentorum, seu sciagraphia* was published as an appendix to the second volume of the author's famous *Syntagma musicum*—a book of extreme rarity. A full bibliographical description of it is printed in Grove, article *Praetorius.*

$6\frac{7}{8}$ in. by $5\frac{1}{4}$ in.

British Museum, London.

Nürmbergisch Geigenwerck.

PLATE XXXIX

" GEIGENWERK "

By Fray Raymundo Truchador

Spanish, 1625.

A REMARKABLE similarity exists between this instrument and the engraving reproduced in the previous plate. The four wheels are in this instance set in motion by a handle at the tail end of the case in such a way that, for every one revolution of the wheel for the lowest bass strings, an increasing number are performed by the other wheels, until the one for the highest treble notes does two and a half. The forty-five gut strings, giving with short octave a compass of four octaves, are brought into contact with the rotating wheels when the keys are pressed down. The maker's signature on the inside of the case is followed by the word *Inventor* which, however, was often used by craftsmen to mean *maker*.

The influence of the Flemish craftsmen, whose instruments went in large quantities to Spain, is reflected in the two sound-holes, the decorations of flowers and foliage on the soundboard, and the paintings on the interior of the lid. The arms of its first owner are embroidered in silk and gold thread on the red velvet which covers the case.

The nationality of this instrument is also signified by the fact that the keyboard is only thirteen inches from the ground, for the Spaniards inherited from their Moorish conquerors, and observed as late as the seventeenth century, the oriental custom of sitting on a cushion on the ground for the performance of music.

Musée Instrumental du Conservatoire, Brussels.

PLATE XL

HARPSICHORD

By John Haward

English, 1622.

In the dressing-room adjoining the Spangle Bedroom at Knole, the historic seat of the Sackvilles, there stands a harpsichord which is not only interesting as a specimen of fine craftsmanship but is also important as it is the earliest known English harpsichord in existence. The lid and most of the action have gone, but the oak case and fine arcaded Renaissance stand testify to the fine workmanship of its maker, whose name appears as JOHANNES (H)A(W)ARD. The erased letters have been supplied by Canon Galpin and there can be little doubt that this was an earlier member of the famous Haward family of the second half of the century. He may, perhaps, also be identified with the John Haward mentioned by Mace (*Musick's Monument*, p. 235) as being the inventor of the pedal-harpsichord:

an *Instrument* of a *Late Invention,* contriv'd (as I have been inform'd) by one Mr. *John Hayward* of *London,* a most *Excellent Kind of Instrument for a Consort.* . . . This *Instrument* (call'd the *Pedal* because It is contriv'd to give *Varieties* with the *Foot*) . . . is in *Shape and Bulk* just like a *Harpsicon*; only It differs in the *Order* of It, Thus, *viz.* There is made right underneath the *Keys,* near the *Ground,* a kind of *Cubbord,* or *Box,* . . . in which *Box* the *Performer* sets *both his Feet* . . . There being right underneath his Toes 4 little *Pummels of Wood* . . . so that thus you may perceive he has several *Various Stops* at Pleasure; and all *Quick and Nimble,* by the *Ready Turn* of the Foot. . . . I caus'd one of *Them* to be made in my *House,* that has 9 several other *Varieties* (24 in all) by reason of a *Stop* (to be *Slip'd* in with the *Hand*) which my *Work-man* calls the *Theorboe-Stop*; and indeed It is not much unlike It; But what It wants of a *Lute,* It has in Its own *Singular Prittiness.*

This is the earliest English reference to the lute stop which was so popular in the following century.

Length, 8 ft. 4 in.; width, 2 ft. 10 in.

Lord Sackville.

120

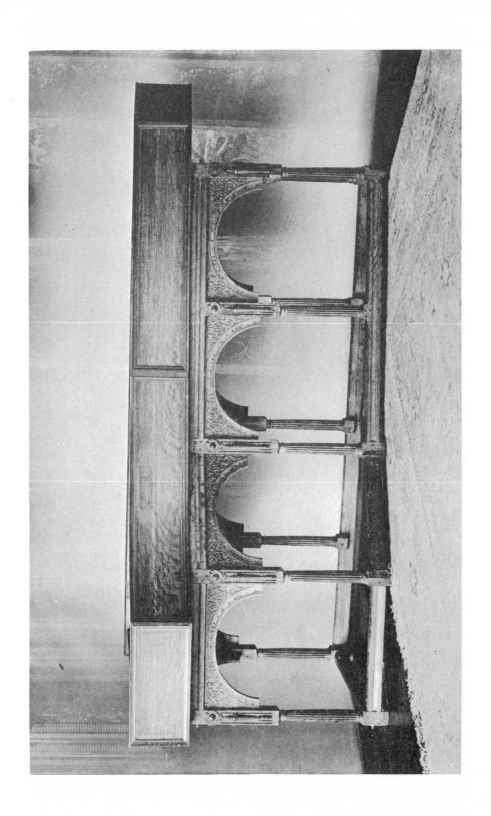

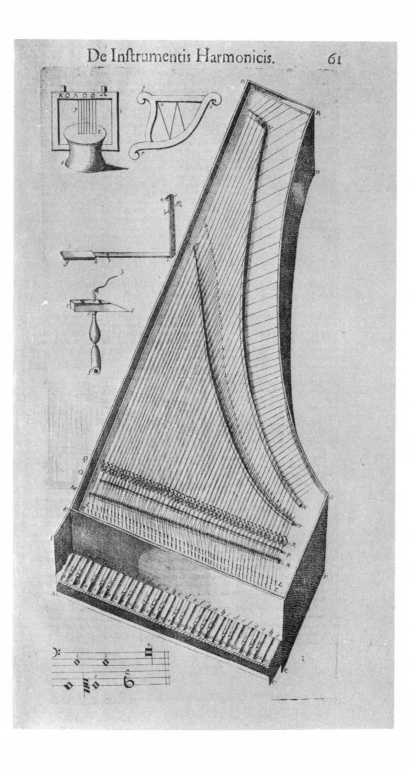

PLATE XLI

ENGRAVING OF A HARPSICHORD

Paris, 1635.

WITH the arrival of the seventeenth century musical literature shows a great advance both in scope and style from the nebulous and inaccurate works of the early writers. The *El Melopeo* of Pedro Cerone and the works of Père Marin Mersenne especially, if fantastic and long-winded, are worthy of note for their descriptions of the instruments then in use. Mersenne, the friend of Descartes, Pascal, and Peiresc, has a voluminous list of publications to his credit on mathematical, theological, and scientific subjects, but his chief interest lay in music. After publishing several small books on musical subjects he produced in 1635 his *Harmonicorum Libri XII*, in a single folio volume. The last four books contain descriptions and numerous woodcuts and engravings of the contemporary instruments.

The engraving of a harpsichord reproduced here is very accurately drawn. It has no stops and only two strings to each note, one unison and one octave. As each key is lettered we can see that the bottom octave is chromatic and not short. By the side of the harpsichord the engraver has depicted a tuning-hammer, and a key-lever on which rests a jack showing the pivoted tongue in which the quill-point is fixed (see p. 21). The tuning-hammer performs the triple duty of knocking in the wrest-pins, making a loop at one end of the string by means of the small hook, and screwing up the wrest-pins—the end of the handle acting as a key—to tune each note. The curious stringed instruments at the top of the plate are, the author tells us, taken from old coins and are supposed to represent the psalteries of the ancients from which he traces the harpsichord's descent!

The plates in this work were also used for Mersenne's *magnum opus*, which he brought out the following year under the title *Harmonie Universelle*. Many of them were again copied by the famous Jesuit, Athanasius Kircher, in his *Musurgia Universalis*, which was published at Rome in 1650.

Royal College of Music, London.

PLATE XLII

HARPSICHORD

By Andreas Ruckers

Antwerp, 1651.

VIEWED from above this instrument shows the fine proportions, graceful outline, and arrangement of the soundboard of the harpsichord. The very naturalistic paintings on the soundboard—a form of decoration specially associated with the Ruckers family—are also clearly visible. These include a concert of monkeys and the date of the instrument, which can be seen close to the sound-hole containing the maker's ornamental mark and initials. The black japanned deal case and the interior ornamentation of gold flowers and conventional Latin mottoes on a red ground are original. The inscriptions are: on the inside of the lid, *Sic transit gloria mundi*; on the folding flap of the lid, *Musica donum Dei*; and on the nameboard *Andreas Ruckers me fecit Antwerpiae 1651*. The keys are modern and the original compass has been extended in the bass, thus abolishing the short octave—an alteration which was made on many Ruckers instruments in the eighteenth century (see p. 44). The crank levers with brass knobs at the end projecting through the nameboard were also a later improvement for the control of the stops, which were originally moved by slides projecting through the right-hand side of the case (see Pl. XXXVII). This change is probably to be attributed to a Dutch musician named Quirin Van Blankenburg (b. 1654) whose valuable information about the Ruckers instruments in his *Elementa musica* (1739) has been carefully discussed by Hipkins (pp. 81 *ff.*). His claim to have invented the lute stop can hardly be admitted, however, in view of the passage in *Musick's Monument* in which a " Theorboe-Stop " is described (see Pl. XL).

This instrument has the usual three sets of strings, two unison (8 ft. tone) and one octave (4 ft. tone). The lower keyboard acts on all three and the upper on one unison set only; but the two unison stops can be withdrawn from the lower keyboard by pressure on the two knobs on the left of the nameboard.

Additional interest is given to this harpsichord by its connection with Handel. Documentary evidence of its identification with the " large harpsichord " which the composer bequeathed, together with £2000, to his friend Christopher Smith, the father of one of his amanuenses, has been produced (Engel, p. 279). But the same claim has been made for another harpsichord by Hans Ruckers the elder in the possession of His Majesty the King. As this instrument is nearly a foot longer than the one reproduced here, and as Smith is known to have bequeathed many of Handel's manuscript scores, his bust by Roubiliac, and his harpsichord to George III in gratitude for the continuance of a pension, its claim seems equally strong. Nor must we forget that Handel had a Shudi harpsichord (see p. 42) which would have been still " larger," and might well be the instrument given to Christopher Smith.

Length, 6 ft. 8 in.; width, 3 ft.

Victoria and Albert Museum, London.

PLATE XLIII

HARPSICHORD

By Vincent Tibaut

French, 1679.

THIS beautiful instrument is in a remarkable state of preservation and is in its original condition. The walnut marquetry case is of unusual richness, especially the inside of the lid. The soundboard is painted with sprays of flowers and has a gilt rose. It is signed in marquetry on the nameboard: *Fait par moy Vincent Tibaud à Tolose,* 1679. At each end of the two rows of keys is a carved lion. It rests upon a stand with eight spiral legs. The apparent compass of each keyboard is four octaves and a semitone, B-C, but this is extended by short octave to G, making four octaves and a fourth, the two lowest sharps being divided. The three rows of jacks with leather plectra which act on two unison strings and an octave are all operated by the lower keyboard: while the upper keyboard acts on one of the unison strings. There are an octave and a unison stop.

Length, 6 ft. $9\frac{1}{2}$ in.; width, 2 ft. 6 in.; height, 3 ft.

Musée Instrumental du Conservatoire Royal, Brussels.

PLATE XLIV

HARPSICHORD

By Thomas Hitchcock

English, c. 1690.

ALTHOUGH several spinets by Thomas and John Hitchcock have survived, there are only two harpsichords: one by John, which is at Lyme Park, Cheshire, and one by Thomas, which is illustrated in this plate. It is of the unusually high quality of craftsmanship which characterizes all their instruments. The sharps are inlaid with slips of ivory—a fashion started by Thomas Hitchcock; the lid is fitted with four strap hinges of brass which are very finely engraved; and the walnut case is gracefully curved at the " tail " end. The name-board is signed *Thomas Hitchcock fecit Londini,* but there is no number. The first key-lever bears the interesting inscription in ink *James D: Harpsichord.* The letter *D* signifies a double harpsichord. This is clear evidence of the employment of other crafts-men by the Hitchcocks, and therefore of the firm's prosperity. A spinet in the Bethnal Green Museum signed by Thomas Hitchcock (No. 1484) was also made by " James," being inscribed in a contemporary hand *James* [*h*]*is No. 4;* and the harpsichord by John Hitchcock at Lyme Park is similarly inscribed *Sam's No. 3 Double three stops, i.e.* it had two keyboards and three stops. This method of signature by craftsmen was often used during the eighteenth century, especially in the case of those employed by dealers, whose names often appear on the name-board although they did not make the instrument.

Much confusion has been caused by the numbers which they gave their instruments: these are often inscribed on the name-board and are easily mistaken for dates. The highest number known on an instrument by Thomas is 1547. John evidently took charge of the business soon after and continued the numerical sequence, as a spinet numbered 1625 bears his signature. The instrument numbered 1676, also a spinet, formerly belonged to Handel and is now preserved at the Royal College of Music, London. The highest number yet discovered is 2012, which is also on a spinet.

Length, 7 ft. 8 in.; width, 3 ft. 1 in.; height, 2 ft. 10 in.

Victoria and Albert Museum, London.

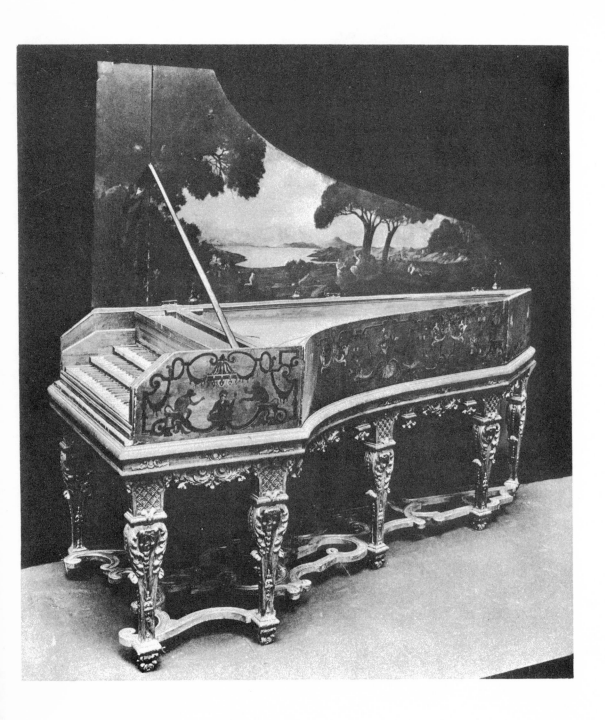

PLATE XLV

HARPSICHORD WITH THREE KEYBOARDS

Italian, c. 1700.

It is known that there were harpsichords with three keyboards in the seventeenth and eighteenth centuries, but they seem never to have established themselves in the favour of musicians. The lack of references to them in contemporary literature is as marked as the dearth of surviving examples, all of which are of Italian workmanship (see also p. 44). There is one in the Metropolitan Museum, New York, made by Vincenzo Sodi of Florence and dated 1779: another in the museum at Wurtemberg is dated 1602 (?) and was made by Simone Remoti. The maker of the instrument in this plate is unknown.

The absence of stops in these instruments suggests the chief reason for the construction of three keyboards, which are usually so made that the octave strings are controlled by the upper manual, the unison and the octave by the middle, and the two unisons by the lower.

The only representation of one of these harpsichords is in a French coloured etching (Pl. LI). In addition to a brief reference in Mersenne's *Harmonie Universelle* (Livre 3e, Proposition XXI) there is an interesting passage in Marpurg's *Historisch-Kritischen Beyträge* (Berlin, 1757) in which he describes a " three-rowed " harpsichord which has three unisons, an octave, and a double lute-stop (whatever that might be) which gave fifteen varieties of tone. The lower keyboard was used for Preludes and Accompaniments, the middle one for Concerts and Solos, and the top for an Echo.

MM. M. & A. Salomon.

125

PLATE XLVI A AND B

FOLDING HARPSICHORD

By Jean Marius

French, 1715.

Marius, who is remembered for his unsuccessful claims to the invention of the piano (see p. 50), also applied his inventive genius to the harpsichord and produced the *clavecin brisé ou de voyage*, of which at least five examples are extant. He obtained a patent on the 18th September 1700 for a period of twenty years, and most of these instruments bear his official stamp on the soundboard, encircled by the words EXCLUSIF PRIVILEGE DU ROI. The instrument is a small harpsichord, made without a stand or legs, and divided into three sections (Fig. *a*). The right-hand section is joined at its apex by a hinge to the middle section and rotates in the same plane on the hinge till the keys are opposite those of the middle section, thus forming two sections of equal length. The longest part then folds over on top of these two making an oblong box (Fig. *b*). The keys are pushed in below the wrest-pins. The compass is four octaves and a fourth, B-E, being extended by short octave, and the lowest D$^\sharp$ is divided (see p. 31). There are two unison strings to each note.

In addition to this instrument belonging to MM. Salomon, the strings of which are gone, there are other examples, to which the above description applies, preserved at Paris (Chouquet, p. 46), Brussels (Brussels Catalogue, No. 555), and Leipzig (Kinsky, p. 100). The last two are dated 1709 and 1713 respectively, and the Leipzig instrument has a set of octave strings as well as the two unisons. There is also one at Berlin of smaller compass (B-C, lowest C$^\sharp$ divided) which belonged to Frederick the Great and is said to have been used by him on his travels.

Length, 4 ft. 5 in.; width, 2 ft. 5 in.

MM. M. & A. Salomon.

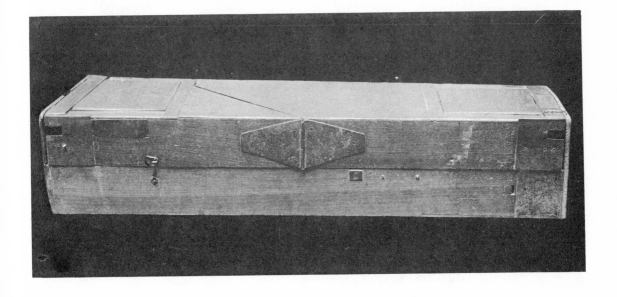

PLATE XLVII

HARPSICHORD

By a member of the Ruckers family

Flemish, first half of the XVIIth century. Decorated in France, c. 1735.

ALL the decorative styles of the eighteenth century—Rococo, Classicism, and Chinoiserie—which were employed for the embellishment of furniture were also adapted to the keyboard instruments. In France especially, the cases and stands of the instruments were enriched with the most lavish decorations. The cases were often covered with the popular *vernis Martin*, and the lids were sometimes painted by Watteau, Boucher, and other favourite artists (see p. 44, note 3).

The Ruckers' instruments, prized for their wonderful tone, were often treated in this manner after they had been extended in compass. It must have been just such another instrument as we illustrate here that Dr. Burney saw on his tour through France:

> After church M. Balbastre invited me to his house, to see a fine Rucker harpsichord which he has had painted inside and out with as much delicacy as the finest coach or even snuff-box I ever saw at Paris. On the outside is the birth of Venus; and on the inside of the cover the story of Rameau's most famous opera, Castor and Pollux; earth, hell, and elysium are there represented: in elysium, sitting on a bank, with a lyre in his hand is that celebrated composer himself; the portrait is very like, for I saw Rameau in 1764. The tone of this instrument is more delicate than powerful; one of the unisons is of buff, but very sweet and agreeable; the touch very light, owing to the quilling, which in France is always weak.

Claud Balbastre was one of the most famous French organists of the century and an ardent admirer of the harpsichord. He had no belief in the future of the piano and said to Pascal Taskin, when he started making pianos, " Vous aurez beau faire. Jamais ce nouveau ne détrônera le majestueux clavecin."

PLATE XLVIII

PORTRAIT OF SHUDI AND HIS FAMILY

Artist unknown, c. 1744.

WE learn from Shudi's biographer that this group was executed for, and remained for 120 years in, a space in the panelling over the fire-place in the front parlour of his house in Great Pulteney Street, to which he moved in 1742 (Dale, pp. 42-4). In it the famous craftsman in a blue dressing-gown is seated tuning a harpsichord while his elder son Joshua in a blue coat stands at his side. His first wife, in a yellow silk gown, is seated on a chair with a newspaper in her right hand. Her younger son Burkat, clothed in a red coat, leans against her left knee while she puts her left arm round him. On the wall behind the instrument are hanging a landscape and the engraved portraits of Frederick, Prince of Wales, and his wife Augusta, Princess of Wales. The Prince was one of Shudi's patrons, and for him was made, in 1740, the double keyboard harpsichord now at Windsor Castle.

Many opinions have been expressed about the identity of the unknown artist who painted this charming conversation piece. The names of George Knapton and Philip Mercier, a German of French extraction, have been suggested, and of the two the latter is the more likely in view of the style. The picture is finely composed and the drawing and modelling are of excellent quality, but the colouring has a certain hardness. Mercier, who lived in the same street as Shudi, painted the Earl of Malmesbury's portrait of Handel and was also patronized by the Prince of Wales.

The instrument in the picture is traditionally stated to have been presented by Shudi to Frederick the Great in gratitude for his victory at the battle of Prague, but it cannot be traced to-day. He certainly made two harpsichords in 1766 for Frederick, which are now in the Neues Palais, Potsdam.

32 in. by 55½ in.

Capt. Evelyn Broadwood.

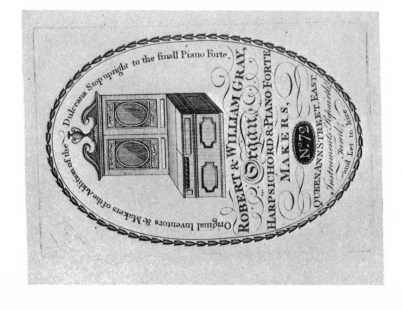

PLATE XLIX A AND B

TRADE-CARDS

(*a*) ROBERT AND WILLIAM GRAY

c. 1795.

(*b*) SAMUEL BLUMER

c. 1745.

THE engraved trade-cards of the eighteenth century form an interesting study and have been made the subject of a recent book by Mr. Ambrose Heal (*London tradesmen's cards of the XVIII century*, 1925). They often contain, as in this case, valuable historical details in addition to interesting pictorial representations of the trade being carried on. Here (*b*) we see Blumer tuning a harpsichord for the benefit of a lady and gentleman who are, doubtless, prospective customers. The costumes and the characteristic rococo frame belong to the Seventeen Forties, and a bill-head with the same engraving is dated 22nd August 1753 (Dale, p. 51). The reference to his former employer, the famous Shudi, was presumably intended to set a seal upon the standard of his craftsmanship—a practice not unknown to-day: it also reminds us that they both came from Switzerland and probably—as Dale suggests—from the same town, *i.e.* Schwanden. None of his instruments have survived so far as is known at present, but amongst the objects offered for sale in *The World*, 12th January 1788, is a " capital double-keyed Harpsichord, one of Blumer's best make and cost 46 guineas."

(*a*) $3\frac{5}{8}$ in. by $2\frac{1}{2}$ in.; (*b*) 6 in. by $4\frac{1}{2}$ in.

(*a*) *Mr. Ambrose Heal.*
(*b*) *Mr. Arthur F. Hill, F.S.A.*

PLATE L

HARPSICHORD

By Jacob Kirkman

English, 1761.

ENGLISH harpsichord-makers of the eighteenth century were content with, and their patrons in the ordinary way demanded, nothing more than plain cases of walnut or mahogany with brass strap-hinges, which formed a striking contrast with the lavishly decorated continental instruments. We must, however, except a group of four harpsichords, and perhaps more, made by Jacob Kirkman, all of which are profusely decorated with marquetry on the inside of the case and with a checky banding of inlay on the lid and the outside of the case. The rather heavy style of the marquetry probably denotes German craftsmanship, and it is not unlikely that Kirkman employed a fellow-countryman for this part of the work. The stands have cabriole legs terminating in claw-and-ball feet.

This harpsichord has the usual compass of five octaves, F-F, and four stops—the lute and octave on the left of the nameboard and the two unisons on the right. There is no harp stop, but it would have come first on the extreme left of the nameboard in accordance with Kirkman's usual arrangement of the stops. The order on Shudi's instruments is different, the lute stop being on the extreme left, then the octave and harp (see p. 132).

The three other harpsichords of similar appearance are at Padworth House (1755), Nostell Priory (1766), and Warley Place, Essex (1766). The last of these was made to the order of George III for Queen Charlotte who, being an accomplished musician, wanted an up-to-date harpsichord in place of her instrument by Jean Ruckers, which is now preserved in the Victoria and Albert Museum.

Length, 7 ft. 8½ in.; width, 3 ft. 1 in.

Mr. Arthur F. Hill, F.S.A.

PLATE LI

COLOURED ETCHING

BY SIGMUND FREUDEBERG

French, c. 1768.

THE work of the French engravers of the eighteenth century, like that of the Dutch painters of the previous century, is of immense value in a study of contemporary life and manners. The idle aristocracy of the one age devoted as much time to music as the hard-working bourgeoisie of the other; and in this very rare coloured etching, which is entitled *La Leçon de clavecin*, we have the counterpart of a canvas by Steen, Metsu, Vermeer and many others to whom the subject was equally dear. Freudeberg (1745-1801) was a Swiss who went to Paris in 1765, where he lived intermittently studying under Boucher, Greuze, and other artists.

Additional interest is given to this print by the presence of a harpsichord with three manuals (*clavecin à trois claviers*), especially as documentary evidence of the existence of these instruments is confined to two short references in the works of Mersenne and Marpurg (see p. 125). Surviving examples are of great rarity, and some of them are of very doubtful authenticity.

226 mm. by 183 mm.

Bibliothèque Nationale, Paris.

131

PLATE LII

HARPSICHORD

By Burkat Shudi and John Broadwood

English, 1773.

ADDITIONAL interest is attached to this harpsichord inasmuch as it was made for the Empress Maria Theresa. We learn from the diary and account-book kept by Barbara Broadwood that it was despatched on 20th August 1773 (Dale, p. 67). This happened to be the day after Shudi died, but the partnership was continued by his son Burkat. The following inscription is on the nameboard: *Burkat Shudi et Johannes Broadwood, Londini, fecerunt. No. 691.* The mahogany case is banded with satinwood and has the usual strap hinges, but the stand is more elaborately carved than usual. The enlarged compass of five octaves and a fourth also proclaims that it is a special instrument. The arrangement of stops and pedals is that usually adopted by Shudi, and as it is typical of the harpsichord at its finest period in England, a detailed description follows. There are three strings for each note, two unison of eight-foot tone and one octave of four-foot tone; and there are four rows of jacks operated by two keyboards. Each row of jacks is kept in position by a rack through which they move up and down, and each rack can be given a sideways movement (operated by the stops described below) which causes the plectra of the jacks to miss the strings. The lower keyboard works the three rows of jacks farthest removed from it; the upper one works the fourth row, which acts on the first unison string but at a point much nearer the keyboard; it also works on the second unison string. There are five stops on the nameboard, three on the left, and two on the right. Starting from the left their names and functions are as follows:

1. The lute stop. This controls the fourth row of jacks described above. It takes its name from the reedy quality of tone due to the unusual harmonies caused by the position of the node, *i.e.* near the end of the string. It was sometimes called the guitar stop.

2. The octave stop. The octave strings are stretched underneath the two unison strings, and being shorter have their own bridges.

3. The harp stop. Also called the buff stop because it mutes the second unison strings by bringing a sliding rack of small leather pads into contact with them. The lower keyboard must be used with this stop.

4. First unison stop.

5. Second unison stop.

There is also a sixth stop called the " machine " on the inside of the case to the left of the keyboard. It is used in conjunction with the left pedal which—when the stop has been previously set—with pressure from the foot brings the lute stop into action on the upper keyboard and the buff on the lower.

The right foot pedal raises the Venetian swell, so called from its obvious resemblance to the blind of that type. This contrivance for obtaining a *crescendo* was patented by Shudi in 1769, although he had used it three years earlier: it was successfully transferred to the organ and was added to other harpsichords when the patent expired. This illustration shows the Venetian swell fully open.

Length, 8 ft. 9¾ in.; width, 3 ft. 4 in.; height, 3 ft. 2 in.

Musée Instrumental du Conservatoire Royal, Brussels.

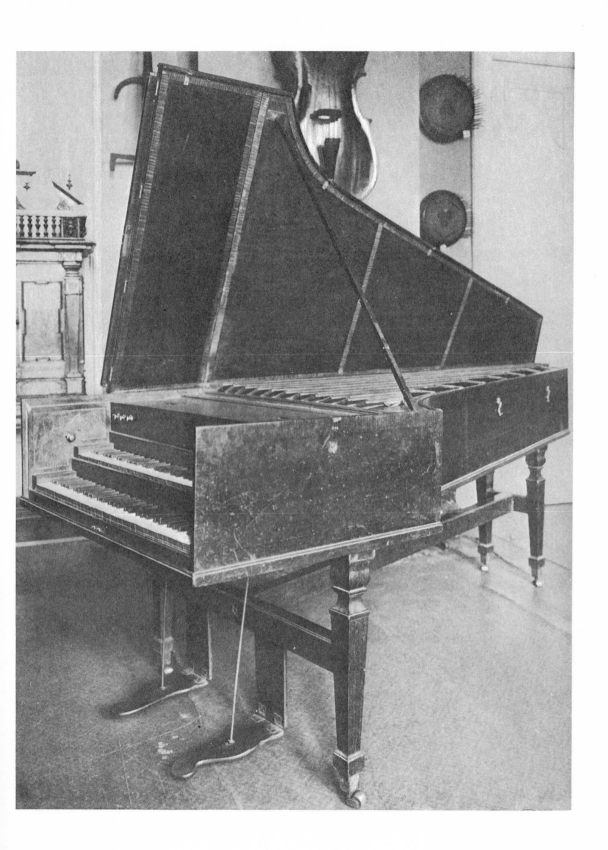

Ralph
1774.

Sketched for the Temple of Hygeia.

PLATE LIII

ORIGINAL DESIGN OF A HARPSICHORD FOR CATHERINE, EMPRESS OF RUSSIA

By Robert Adam

Inscribed: Adelphi, 1774.

THE Sir John Soane Museum contains a famous collection of drawings and designs by Robert Adam, and in a portfolio there two delicately coloured drawings may be seen of a harpsichord and a square piano for Catherine, Empress of Russia. It is the first of these that is reproduced here, and while it was probably executed by one of Adam's draughtsmen, there can be little doubt that he himself added the bolder pen-strokes, strengthening the drawing of the satyrs in the stand. It was engraved and figured in *The Works in Architecture* (vol. i, 1778), where it is described as a " Design of a Harpsichord inlaid with various-coloured woods executed in London for the Empress of Russia." A glance reveals that Adam cannot have been a musician, for the position of the keyboard in the centre of the case makes the instrument quite impracticable. Indeed, the following significant words are added to the description in the above-mentioned work: " This design was considerably altered by the person who executed the work."

Sir John Soane Museum, London.

133

PLATE LIV

HARPSICHORD

By Jean Couchet

Antwerp, c. 1645, restored by Pascal Taskin in 1783-4, and re-decorated about that date.

THE important improvements to the harpsichord made by Jean Couchet, the nephew of Jean Ruckers, have already been described (see p. 37). This instrument is one of the very rare surviving examples of his craftsmanship and, in common with many of the Ruckers' instruments, was restored by the famous French harpsichord-maker Pascal Taskin in the eighteenth century. Evidence of Taskin's restorations are frequently found in the Parisian periodical entitled *Affiches, annonces et avis divers, e.g.*

Clavecin de Couchet refait à neuf et mis à grand rav. par P. Taskin, avec des peintures précieuses et mécaniques au pied pour varier le jeu de 10 à 12 manières.

This entry might well refer to such an instrument as this, except that the case, with its Louis Seize stand, is decorated not with paintings, but with black and red lacquer, with figures and scenes in gold, in imitation of the Chinese—a decorative style much favoured at this date; and the pedals are of modern construction, having been substituted by Mr. Dolmetsch for the original handstops. Taskin's restoration is signified by the two following inscriptions: *Refait par Pascal Taskin à Paris* 1784, and on the nameboard *Fait par Pascal Taskin à Paris* 1783. This consisted of an extension of the compass by the abolition of the old short octave and a small increase in the size of the soundboard. The operation was usually termed *grand ravalement* and is referred to in an abbreviated form in the extract quoted above. Couchet followed the Ruckers in putting a gilt rose in the sound hole. His device consists of a seated female figure playing the harp between the letters I C, and has been preserved in this harpsichord. The four pedals operate the two unison stops, the octave, and a harp stop. There is no lute stop. An unusual feature is the sliding in and out of the top keyboard so that it can be put out of action at will.

Of the few surviving harpsichords by this maker we can mention one at the Metropolitan Museum, New York (Cat., p. 89); one at Brussels (No. 276) which is dated 1646; and one which was sold in New York in the Freund sale (Anderson Galleries, 25-28 March 1925). The last of these was also restored by Taskin in 1781. Grove (article *Harpsichord*) tells us that there is one " in Edinburgh." There is a double keyboard spinet—a very rare type of instrument —by him dated 1640 in the Boers collection at the Rijksmuseum, Amsterdam. Couchet entered the Guild of St. Luke in 1642 and died in 1655. He was succeeded by his son P. E. Jean Couchet, who carried on the business, and entered the Guild in 1696. Another older son, or a nephew, named Joseph was also an instrument-maker and entered the Guild in 1665, and in the following year an Abraham Couchet was admitted.

Mrs. George Crawley.

PLATE LV

HARPSICHORD

By Pascal Taskin

French, 1786.

Pascal Taskin was the founder and most distinguished member of a family of instrument-makers of this name. He was born at Theux, in the province of Liège, in 1723, but migrated to Paris, where he was apprenticed to, and eventually succeeded, Etienne Blanchet, whose harpsichords were renowned for their lightness of touch. Taskin is chiefly remembered for his re-introduction, in 1768, of leather (*peau de buffle*) in place of the usual crow-quill for the jacks of the harpsichord. He also was an expert in restoring and enlarging the fine old Flemish instruments of the previous century. His activities in this direction are described on the preceding plate. He was official instrument-maker to Marie Antoinette, but he refused to accept the guardianship of the King's instruments (see Grove, article *Taskin*). He died in 1793.

This elegant *clavecin* was evidently made for a lady, as the keys are exceptionally narrow, and it rests upon a Louis Seize stand of richly carved and gilt wood. The case is lacquered in imitation of the Chinese style, and the soundboard is painted with flowers. The compass is five octaves and one note, each note having two unison strings. Either of these can be silenced by a stop, and there is a harp stop. The obvious restoration of this instrument, including the substitution of quills for Taskin's leather plectra, is confirmed by the following inscription in ink on the back of the nameboard: *Refait par Charles Fleury facteur de pianos à Paris an 1856 fleury.*

Length, 6 ft. 1 in.; width, 2 ft. 7 in.; height, 2 ft. 9½ in.

Victoria and Albert Museum, London.

PLATE LVI

PIANOFORTE

By Bartolomeo Cristofori

Italian, 1720.

THIS historic instrument is the earlier of the two surviving pianos made by Cristofori and is, therefore, the oldest piano in existence: the other, which is dated 1726, is in the Leipzig University collection and is illustrated in Kinsky's catalogue (p. 171). The close resemblance of the instrument to a typical Italian *clavicembalo* must be noticed. The shape and size, the characteristic battens on the side of the case, the survival of the jack-rail, the arcaded fronts of the keys, etc., all suggest that these first pianos were merely harpsichords with a hammer action in place of the usual jacks, although there is no doubt that they were definitely constructed as pianos and were not converted (see p. 48).

This instrument is now preserved in the Metropolitan Museum, New York, and the following details of its construction are to be found in the catalogue of keyboard instruments (p. 122). The compass is four octaves and a fourth, B-E, the stringing being bichord and the vibrating length of the longest string 6 ft. 2 in., and of the shortest $4\frac{1}{2}$ in. The ivory knobs on the blocks at each end of the keyboard keep the action in place and enable it to be taken out when they are removed. Above the nameboard on the block is the following inscription: *Bartholomaeus de Christophoris Patavinus Inventor Faciebat Florentiae MDCCXX.*

Length, 7 ft. 7 in.; width, 3 ft. 3 in.; depth, $9\frac{1}{2}$ in.

Metropolitan Museum of Art, New York.

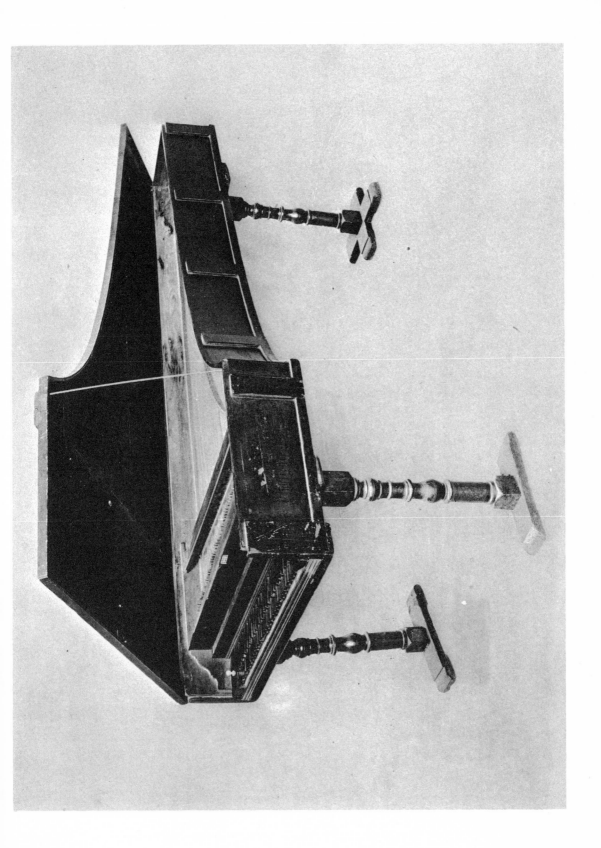

PLATE LVII

SQUARE PIANOFORTE

By Johann Christoph Zumpe

English, 1767.

The circumstances relating to Zumpe's introduction of the square piano into England and the action of his instruments have already been fully described (pp. 51-2). But it is interesting to note that, except for an experimental instrument made for Dr. Crotch in the previous year which has seventeen notes to the octave and which is now in Messrs. J. Broadwood's collection, this is the earliest surviving piano made by him. It is dated 1767 and has the number XVIIII chiselled on the back of the nameboard, and, when the action was recently removed for repair, the same number was found to be scratched or pencilled on various other parts of the inside of the case. It has hitherto been maintained that this signifies that it was the nineteenth instrument from his shop, but this is hardly possible if he began making pianos in 1761. Also, Rimbault refers (p. 132) to another of these pianos made in 1768 " with the mark XVIII upon it which appears to be the number he had then made." It is far more likely that these numbers were scratched on each piece to ensure the correct assemblage of parts. This view is supported by the fact that the demand for these little instruments was so great that Zumpe could not make them fast enough, and had to pass on orders he could not deal with to his countryman Pohlmann. The ubiquity of his pianos is commented upon by Dr. Burney; and their popularity is reflected in a letter from the poet Gray to his friend the Rev. William Mason, poet and composer. He says " You will tell me what to do with your Zumpe, which has amused me much here."

By 1769 Zumpe had been joined by Gabriel Buntebart, thus forming a partnership which was dissolved by mutual consent—so we learn from the *London Gazette*—on the 24th September 1778. He was then joined by Meyer, but by 1785 we find pianos made by Schœne & Co., whose signature on the nameboard is followed by the significant words " successors to Johannes Zumpe." Having realized an ample fortune he then returned to his native country.

Length, 4 ft. 3 in.; width, 1 ft. 6½ in.; depth, 6½ in.

Victoria and Albert Museum, London.

PLATE LVIII

SQUARE PIANOFORTE

By Frederick Beck

English, 1775.

THE person for whom this instrument was made in the first place was evidently intent upon having a decorative piece of furniture rather than a useful musical instrument, for the elaborate case into which the piano is built has no recess for the legs of a player seated before it. It is extensively inlaid with coloured woods, and a herring-bone pattern of harewood and wood lines dyed green: in the middle of the front panel there is a medallion framed in a ribbon-banded metal border representing the Muse Thalia. The piano is of the early type with a compass of five octaves less one note, and the customary dampers above the strings. It is evident that Beck employed a cabinet-maker of very great skill and taste to execute cases on special occasions, for there is another of his square pianos dated 1777 (figured in *The Dictionary of English Furniture*, iii, 6), the case of which is certainly by the same hand. In the same work there is an illustration of a commode (vol. ii, 140) on which there is an almost identical medallion undoubtedly executed from the same drawing: this is considered to be " obviously the work of one who had closely studied the Parisian makers." These three notable pieces can therefore be grouped together as the work of one craftsman.

Length, 5 ft. 4 in.; width, 2 ft. 8½ in.; height, 3 ft. 4 in.

By permission of the Trustees of the Lady Lever Collection, Port Sunlight.

PLATE LIX

PIANOFORTE

IN THE FORM OF A SEMICIRCULAR SIDE-TABLE

English, c. 1785.

THE action of the square piano was sometimes adapted to, and built into, cases of various shapes during the last quarter of the eighteenth century, when the contemporary furniture reached the highest degree of elegance. We know of two instances of co-operation between an eminent furniture-designer and the instrument-maker (see Pls. LIII and LXII), and in this case, although the names of both the cabinet-maker and the instrument-maker are unknown, the craftsmanship is of the first order.

This piano is one of a pair constructed to resemble semi-elliptical side-tables. The case is veneered with mahogany and satinwood, and the legs, which have satinwood blocks, are veneered with amboyna. A section of the frieze is hinged and turns back to disclose the keyboard, which is of the usual compass of five octaves. There is a small Venetian swell which is operated by a *genouillère*.

Length, 5 ft. 2 in.

Mr. G. D. Hobson, M.V.O.

PLATE LX

SQUARE PIANO

By Longman & Broderip

English, c. 1790.

The cases of English pianos were sometimes decorated with paintings when this form of embellishment for furniture became fashionable towards the end of the eighteenth century; but it is not often that such fine quality of painting is found on musical instruments as we see on this square piano. The swags of flowers on the front are also carried on to the sides, and the top is elaborately decorated in a similar style.

An oval enamel plaque on the nameboard, often found on pianos during the last fifteen years of the century, bears the makers' names. Longman & Broderip (see p. 53) were, however, not actual makers but dealers in all kinds of instruments, music, etc. Many of their instruments exist to-day.

Length, 5 ft. 2 in.; width, 1 ft. 10 in.; height, 2 ft. 8 in.

Capt. L. Twiston Davies.

PLATE LXI

GRAND PIANOFORTE

Viennese, c. 1795.

THIS is a typical example of the Viennese piano with its square tapering legs, black naturals and white semitones, and *genouillères*. The compass is five octaves and a half, F-C, and the two top octaves are trichord. In place of pedals there are two knee-levers which control the damper action (forte), and the Celeste (piano), which is a thin strip of cloth inserted between the hammers and the strings. This device, invented by the famous maker Stein (see p. 54), was approved by Mozart who, in the well-known letter about Stein's pianos, written to his father, says:

> He has, too, improved the contrivance for exerting pressure by the knee. I can put it in action by the lightest touch and, when one slackens the pressure a little, there is no trace of an echo.

Another maker patronized by Mozart was Anton Walter, and the instrument made by him for the composer is now preserved in the Mozarteum at Salzburg (figured in Grove, Pl. lix).

The piano reproduced here, which is not unlike Mozart's instrument, is traditionally stated to have come from the castle belonging to the Counts of Oppersdorff, near Ober-Glogau, and to have been used by Beethoven when, in company with Prince Lichnowsky, he visited Count Franz von Oppersdorff in 1806. Beethoven dedicated his Fourth Symphony to him.

Length, 6 ft. 7 in.; width, 3 ft. 6 in.; height, 2 ft. 9½ in.

Messrs. Rushworth & Dreaper, Liverpool.

141

PLATE LXII

ENGRAVED DESIGN BY THOMAS SHERATON FOR A GRAND PIANOFORTE

English, 1796.

THE harpsichord and square pianoforte made for Catherine, Empress of Russia, from Robert Adam's original drawings (Pl. LIII), and the grand piano made by John Broadwood's firm for Don Manuel de Godoy, Prime Minister of Spain, from this design by Thomas Sheraton are the only known instruments that have been planned by the famous furniture-designers of the eighteenth century.

The piano, to which Dale devotes the last chapter of his monograph on Shudi, was given by Godoy, or the Prince of the Peace as he was commonly called, to the Queen of Spain, with whom his relations were notoriously intimate. It cost just over £220, with an additional ten guineas for a miniature portrait of Godoy by Alexander Taylor, which was to be set in the oval space on the name-board. This has unfortunately been removed. In the original account the instrument is described as

> A Grand Pianoforte 6 octaves C to C, in sattinwood case ornamented with different woods with water gilt mouldings and Wedgwood's and Tassie's medallions, etc., The Prince of Peace's arms chased and gilt in burnished gold rich carved frame, etc.

We can see from the design that the case is of the old harpsichord shape, although there are stout tapering legs instead of the older trestle. Sheraton made no provision for pedals which he would have considered to detract from the design, but three were subsequently added.

The instrument became, after many vicissitudes, the property of the late Lord Leverhulme, and on the dispersal of his collections, in 1926, it was acquired by the present owners, Mr. and Mrs. George A. Cluett, Troy, New York.

Length, 8 ft. 3 in.; width, 3 ft. 9 in.; height, 3 ft. ½ in.

Messrs. J. Broadwood & Sons, Ltd.

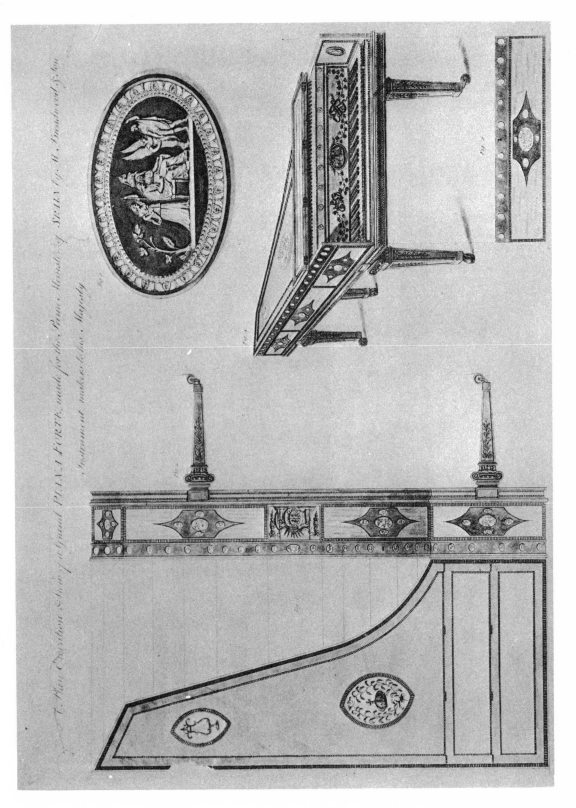

A Plan Elevation & Section of a grand PIANA FORTE, made for the Prince Manders of SPAIN by W. Dashwood & Son.

Instrument makers to his Majesty

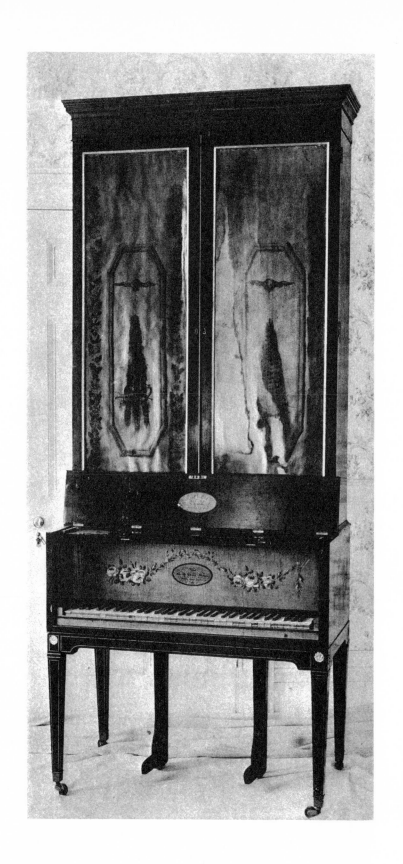

PLATE LXIII

UPRIGHT GRAND PIANOFORTE

By William Stodart

English, 1801.

In the patent granted to Stodart on 12th January 1795, this instrument is described as " an upright grand piano in the form of a bookcase." The " grand principle of action " is stated by the maker to be that " both the hammers and dampers after performing are returned by weight." The action is concealed in a rectangular case, the unoccupied space being fitted with shelves, and there are two glass doors backed with white velvet painted with trophies of musical instruments, etc. The stringing is tricord throughout and the compass is five octaves and a fourth, F-C.

Queen Charlotte possessed one of these instruments which was sold at Christie's on 24th May 1819.

Height, 8 ft. 8 in.; width, 3 ft. 7½ in.; depth, 1 ft. 10 in.

Metropolitan Museum, New York.

PLATE LXIV

UPRIGHT PIANOFORTE

By R. Jones

English, 1808.

THIS instrument was formerly in Carlton House and was evidently made for George IV when he was Prince of Wales. The maker styles himself " Piano Forte Maker to His Royal Highness the Prince of Wales ", and it is not unlikely that the gilt and black Gothic case was made by George Smith, who published a book of designs in the same year as this piano was made which he dedicated to the Prince, describing himself on the title-page as " Upholder Extraordinary to His Royal Highness The Prince of Wales." The decoration is reminiscent of his Gothic style.

The upper part of the case is made in the " bookcase " style introduced by William Stodart (see Pl. LXIII), and has two doors of looking-glass. The compass of six octaves was by this time firmly established.

Height, 9 ft. 1 in.; width, 3 ft. 9 in.; depth, 1 ft. $9\frac{1}{2}$ in.

By gracious permission of His Majesty the King.

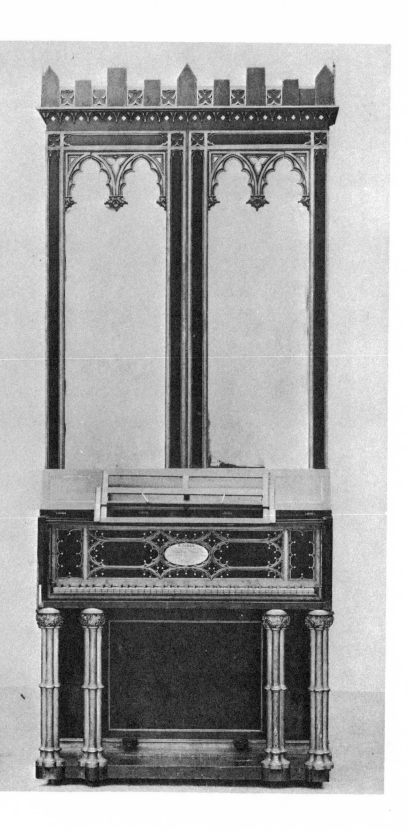

PLATE LXV

CABINET PIANOFORTE

By Van Der Hoef

Amsterdam, c. 1810.

AFTER the introduction of the upright piano action at the beginning of the nineteenth century, instruments were made in various fanciful shapes and decorated in the Empire and Regency styles which were copied from contemporary furniture by instrument-makers at this period. On the Continent, especially in Germany and Austria, pianos of this kind were extremely popular and were made in the shapes signified by such names as *Pyramidenflügel, Lyraflügel,* and the so-called *Giraffenflügel,* which is illustrated in this plate. Only this last type had any vogue in England, where it was made during the second decade of the century, being called the Cabinet-piano. In a contemporary fashion magazine of the year 1812 (R. Ackermann's *Repository of Arts,* vii, 111) an instrument of this kind, made by Wornum & Wilkinson (see the Appendix), is described as

> an instrument of much elegance, with the usual additional keys and pedals. Its height varies from six to seven feet two inches; its width is three feet eight or nine inches; and its projection twenty-one inches. . . . Instruments of this kind, finished in mahogany, are highly ornamental but if in rosewood and brass, they may be pronounced truly superb.

The "usual additional keys" are those that were first added in about 1794, bringing the compass up to six octaves, which was by this time its usual extent.

English makers did not adopt the row of pedals for the production of various unmusical sounds which can be seen in the piano illustrated here—an addition commonly found in the German and Austrian instruments of this date. The number and order of the pedals varied (see Hipkins, p. 110) but we can regard the arrangement followed here as typical. Starting from the left the first pedal, known as the bassoon (*Fagotzug*), brings a slip of parchment into contact with approximately the lowest three octaves; the second operates a drum-stick which hits the belly of the instrument; the third is the celeste soft pedal; the fourth strikes some bells; the fifth is the "shifting" soft pedal which moves the keyboard; and the sixth is the ordinary damper or loud pedal. The case is of mahogany; the capital and base of the Corinthian pillar, the scrolled moulding, and the masks of the lion supports (or monopodia, as they were called) being gilt. The satinwood nameboard is painted with a swag of flowers containing the maker's name. The instrument is represented in the painting entitled "Music, when soft voices die, vibrates in the memory," by Sir William Q. Orchardson, R.A., to whom it formerly belonged.

Greatest height, 7 ft.; width, 4 ft. 8 in.; depth, 2 ft. 3 in.

Bethnal Green Museum, London.

INDEX

The names in the list of makers which form the Appendix are not included unless they are mentioned elsewhere.